THE ADOPTION REUNION

SURVIVAL GUIDE

Preparing Yourself for the Search, Reunion, and Beyond

M.A.

W.

BAKER & TAYLOR

Publisher's Note

Distributed in the U.S.A. by Publishers Group West; in Canada by Raincoast Books; in Great Britain by Airlift Book Company, Ltd.; in South Africa by Real Books, Ltd.; in Australia by Boobook; and in New Zealand by Tandem Press.

Copyright © 2001 by Julie Jarrell Bailey and Lynn Neal Giddens
New Harbinger Publications, Inc.
5674 Shattuck Avenue
Oakland, CA 94609

Cover design by Amy Shoup
Edited by Heather Garnos
Text design by Tracy Marie Powell

Library of Congress Catalog Card Number: 00-134862

ISBN 1-57224-228-0 Paperback

New Harbinger Publications' Web site address: www.newharbinger.com

03   02   01

10   9   8   7   6   5   4   3   2   1

First printing

To my most precious treasures: my daughter Lorna, and my sons, Joshua, Jacob, and Isaac, with unconditional love; to my husband, Steve, for his loving support; and also to my friend Gail Peden, whose reunion touched my heart and changed me forever.

—Julie Jarrell Bailey

For my son, Devin Neal Giddens, the love and light of my life.

—Lynn Neal Giddens

Contents

Part 2
Practical Advice for
Sidestepping Reunion Pitfalls

Part 3
The Tangled Web of Rights and Legal Issues

Part 4
More Help for Your Journey

Foreword

Suddenly, we have become a country besotted with family trees and genealogical searches. We seem to have "come of age" in the year 2000. Although there has been, since our birth as a nation, a small coterie of people who could trace their lineage to the *Mayflower* and her sister ships, and who belonged to the Daughters of the American Revolution or similar organizations, most of our citizens came here in succeeding centuries, leaving family and history behind. They were in a sense reborn as Americans, whose ethnicity was mixed and unimportant. It mattered little in this infant country who your ancestors were. It mattered more what you accomplished on your own. Now, three centuries later, Americans have found a history to research and reclaim. Their families have been separated and spread around the country, and they are eager to locate them, catalogue them, and find themselves a place in this familial tapestry.

It's particularly appropriate that this book, focusing on searches and reunions to reclaim lost connections, is being written and published in the first year of the new century. The authors have gathered together the information and experience of the last three or more decades and distilled them into a meaningful whole. Although searches and reunions have been going on forever, they were furtive and in small numbers. Now, not only have their numbers increased tenfold, but adoptees and birth parents and significant relatives are being aided by government agencies, trained searchers who utilize Internet technology and databases, and adoption agencies that were heretofore reluctant and anti-search. Moreover, new laws have been passed in several states, and are being upheld in the courts, giving adopted people the same right to their original birth certificate as everyone else. The passion for genealogy may be greater in the adoption community than in the general public. But people in search are not generally looking to increase their knowledge of antecedents—they are looking for a person to whom they are genetically related.

Although some other Western countries have tried to emulate the American institution of adoption, our philosophy and practice remain unique for the most part. We need to begin with the recognition that adoption is more widespread in our single nation than in all other nations combined. This phenomenon is directly related to our origins and development as a melting pot, a fruit salad, a melange of different ethnicities. Bloodlines had little meaning or importance here, so taking in a stranger was more acceptable than in other countries where family pride was measured in centuries rather than decades. In the early years of this nation, many orphaned children were shipped from England to join farm families who needed additional help with the land. Some adoptions were legal, others informal, but the sense of being part of a family was forged more easily here than in the old country. Adoption laws were developed to protect those children and offer them safeguards.

Our system is in direct contrast with other countries, other societies. In the Moslem world, adoption is not an option. Instead fostering is the solution for children who need out-of-home placement. Losing one's birth heritage is considered to be unacceptable. In a number of primitive societies, the solution is a type of dual parenting, where the child retains his self-pride through his birth family and gains his nurturing and sustenance through his adoptive or foster family. In France, the original birth certificate is not sealed (except in special cases where the security of the child is at risk), because the child's original identity and family name are considered to be of great importance. A hyphenated adoptive name may be added if all parties agree. Older children are rarely placed for adoption because grandparents have rights to keep children in their family. Other kinds of permanent arrangements are made to meet the needs of the child while maintaining his root connections with kinfolk. In the ancient Judeo-Christian tradition, adoption was considered to be a legal fiction, with stewardship the operative word rather than adoption.

I began my professional role in the institution of adoption midcentury, and for the past five decades, I have been both participant in and witness to the myriad of changes that have taken place. I have been profoundly affected by the emotional reactions of all members of the triad, within themselves and in their interaction with each other. Most poignant and heartrending, I believe, is the experience of reunion and its effect upon everyone involved. The reunion of birthparent and adoptee constructs an unparalleled relationship, and is truly *sui generis*, a totally unique emotional experience. For most experiences, we can compare and contrast with similar situations and therefore make it more understandable and usable. Not so with the reunion experience, and particularly not so with the reunion experience that had its inception in the relinquishment or surrender by the birth mother of a newborn child, followed by the permanent adoptive placement of that child to a stranger couple, complete with sealed records and lifetime expectations of secrecy and anonymity.

Over the years, through my own observations and experience with thousands of members of the triad, as well as the writings of eminent mental health professionals, I have come to believe that closed adoptions have been injurious to the emotional well-being of both adoptees and birth parents. The newborn child is less fully developed than other forms of life. Newborn lambs, calves, puppies, kittens, etc., are up and ambulating within minutes or hours of birth. They wander away from the mother, only to find her by her smell and sound when they need to nurse. Newborn human babies are totally dependent upon their mothers and, when separated bodily, remain as one—united by the familiar heartbeat, voice tones, and smell. This "oneness" is also experienced by the mother whose task is still unfinished in the early weeks after birth. Abrupt separation, it is now accepted, is traumatic for both child and mother. No matter how eager and loving the new adoptive mother is, she does not smell the same or sound the same, nor is her heartbeat familiar to the child. For the birth mother, it is as if a limb has been amputated. It is also now accepted by most mental health professionals that bonding is a physiological process that begins at conception and is with the birth mother only. With the new adoptive mother, there may be strong attachment, but the bonding with the birth mother has been severed and cannot be repaired or replaced by the relationship with the adoptive mother.

Our growing body of literature in the field of adoption is rich with studies and anecdotal material concerning the lifelong pain of triad members. Reunions are a small but significant beginning in the process of healing the wounds of adoptees and birth mothers and replacing both good and bad fantasies with reality. Probably as important for the adoptee is the achievement of basic connections back to a root family, which provides a foundation from which to build an authentic and integrated identity and sense of self. The reunion also deeply concerns adoptive parents, birth fathers, and all the relatives of triad members. Although initially frightening, in the final analysis, the reunion is usually beneficial to all the parties involved because it clarifies ambiguous relationships and dispels amorphous fears. In most situations, reunions do not harm or weaken the adoptive family relationships; to the contrary, the knowledge that the adoptive parents are the real parents, the nurturing parents, becomes obvious and clear to all. This brings us back to the consideration that the relationship of the adoptee and birth parents is special, meaningful, and totally unique.

This clearly written book describes it all, and will give you a special voyage into that complicated world. Reading it will help you navigate those waters and arrive at your destination intact, successful, and rewarded.

—Annette Baran, M.S.W.
Coauthor of *The Adoption Triangle*

Acknowledgments

While adoption always involves loss, the same can be said about acknowledgments. Someone, somewhere, will be inadvertently left off the list, and for that we apologize in advance. When we began writing this book, we were overwhelmed by the outpouring of support and encouragement from members of the adoption community and other friends.

Many people contributed knowingly—and others unwittingly—to this book, and we want to acknowledge their participation. Without them, this reunion guidebook could not have been written. We especially thank the adoptees and birth parents whose stories are shared here. You have touched our lives with your honesty and by sharing such personal issues, and we will forever be grateful for your generosity and courage.

Thank you to all of the authors and pioneers of adoption books: You have served as teachers and friends to us, and you have been a beacon of light in an otherwise dark world that doesn't want to hear that sadness and trauma can exist in adoption. You continue to remind us of our own humanity, or lack of it, and for that, we are truly grateful. A special thanks to our author friends and colleagues: Robert Andersen, M.D., B. J. Lifton, Nancy Newton Verrier, Joyce Maguire Pavao, Ph.D., Randolph Severson, Joe Soll, Ph.D., Annette Baran, Reuben Pannor, Arthur Sorosky, M.D., Christina Crawford, Carol Schaefer, Rickie Sollinger, David Brodzinsky, Francie Portnoy, Jean Strauss, and others. You have been a genuine inspiration to us personally, and to the adoption reform movement universally.

To all of the birth mothers in the world—those we know, as well as those we have not yet met and may never meet—we have heard your silent cries. We hope that you will someday regain your voice and your courage to change the process of adoption, making the need for reunions obsolete. A special thanks to those birth mothers whose voices continue to lead reform: Sandra Musser, Delores Teller, Lee Campbell, and Jane Hart, as well as heartfelt gratitude to birth father and adoption reform leader Fred Greenman. He represents adoption's true silent minority.

We also thank all of the adoptees who have been courageous enough to seek a reunion with their birth family, as well as all of the adoptive parents who continue to support their child's desire to enter a reunion with their birth family. We know your gesture is testimony to all that an open heart can offer. To Jane Nast, Caroline Lindsay, Gail Stern, Rosie Burr, Diane Hogan, Mary DeLaRosa, Jane Barlow, Shirley Geissinger, Faye Hilger, et al., we say keep up the good work. You're an inspiration to prospective adoptive parents everywhere.

There are others, still, who might lack the desire to apply pen to paper with their thoughts on adoption reunions, but are cognizant, articulate, and supportive regardless. Some are our friends in adoption, united in loss, committed to the concept of open records and man's inherent right to knowledge of self. Thank you for sharing your lives, your thoughts, your wisdom, your love, and your patience with us as we dedicated our free time to writing this book. These folks will forever remain close to our hearts: Wanda Howell, Kim Beck, Diana Ricketts, Ray Lewis, Bobbie Baker, Lysle Betts, Darryl Smith, Jeff Chambers, Elaine Franzetti, Curtis Graves, Susan Friel-Williams, and many others.

Beyond adoption, we acknowledge a few longtime friends. Although they aren't members of the adoption triad, they helped us in many ways throughout our independent adoption journeys, both literally and spiritually, their only connection being the compassion and love they held for us over the years. For lending us your strength, your understanding, your forgiveness, and your wide, soft shoulders so many times over the decades, you have endeared yourselves to each of us for eternity and remain steadfast in our hearts and lives: Gail Smith, Mae Horne, Mary Harris, Pearl Sill, Nancy Freeman, Fred Fair, Iris and Bob Faulkner, Nelle and Len Hays, Doug Stenstrom, Carole Ensign, and other friends who have moved on but aren't forgotten. Each of you have had unspoken influences in our lives which in many ways helped mold us into who we are today and we feel that requires acknowledgement. Thank you.

It must also be said that we are most grateful to New Harbinger Publications for their desire to publish this book. We especially want to thank our acquisitions editor, Catharine Sutker. We met by chance and because of her belief in this project, many people will find the support and advice they need to experience a successful reunion.

Also, we especially thank our book editor, Heather Garnos. She was our objective eyes in the writing of this book, keeping us on target and reminding us to come up for air now and again.

Last, but by no means least, we acknowledge our family members, who remained patient and forgiving of us as we missed ballgames, school events, outings, meals, housekeeping, and life in general, in order to complete this book on time. We cherish each of you most in life and there aren't enough good words in the dictionary to describe how we feel about each of you. We love you, Steve, Lorna, Josh, Jacob, Isaac, Devin, our parents, both adoptive and biological, and all of our siblings. Thank you for your energizing support. We hope the completion of the work contained within these pages makes up for our inattentiveness during this past year.

Introduction

Reunions are commonplace in the lives of most people. Reflecting on our youth, many of us remember regular gatherings for family reunions during holidays and summer vacations. Another common form of reunion involves the coming together of old classmates for alumni celebrations or class reunions. When our alma mater organizes a reunion, most of us are excited to again revel in the joys of friendship, memories, and camaraderie with old classmates. Thoughts about approaching class reunions often turn nostalgic as we recall the good old days of a bygone era. The idea of a reunion generally evokes warm feelings and emotions, as well as behaviors that help us recapture something we feel we need to return to, even if only for the magic of the moment.

Adoption-based reunions can stir up similar feelings, although the feelings aren't derived from prior experience or personal familiarity. Feelings and emotions for adoption-based reunions come from a place deep within—a place often indescribable by the participants. These reunions involve a unique magic or illusion.

There are a couple of major reunion obstacles you should be aware of: it's easy to fall prey to unrealistic expectations while approaching the reunion, and it's hard to maintain the new relationship after the reunion. Too many adoptees, birth parents, and other biological family members approach reunion having convinced themselves that they are hosting a family reunion. However, they behave more like they are conducting a class reunion. The difference is that family reunions rely heavily on bloodline familiarity and endure the test of time, while class reunions rely on memories, coupled with old fantasies that may have nothing to do with the present moment.

Because many years have typically passed before the adopted person and the birth parent—statistically, the birth mother—are reunited, it's likely that both have relied on fantasies to block out the uncertainty they feel.

Birth mothers remember the pain and emotions involved in the birthing and relinquishment process. Most (but not all) begin their search looking for the infant they lost years ago. The birth mother remembers the grief she suffered and might still suffer over the loss of the baby she carried in her womb for nine months. She might also suffer from guilt or shame over having been unable to care for her child. Understandably, she may ache to hold that baby in her arms again, not facing the reality that her baby is now an adult.

Adoptees often long to know more about their birth parents, regardless of deciding to search or not search for either one of them. It isn't unusual for an adoptee to spend many hours of his lifetime wondering about his birth family and why he was surrendered for adoption. Sometimes, when he sees a woman or man of the right age, who has similar hair or eye coloring, bone structure, or other likenesses to himself, he might envision them to be related. Adoptees occasionally fantasize that their birth mother or father is someone famous or important, and, likewise, birth parents might envision their infant as having grown up to be a Nobel prize winner, famous actor, politician, or some other very accomplished person. These dreams can be attributed to the belief that something wonderful must have occurred as the result of such a great sacrifice.

Adoptive parents who were given little or no information about their child's biological history often add to the problem as they try to comfort their child with embellishments about the birth family. The birth mother, desiring to place her baby in an affluent home to guarantee a happier, more secure future than she can provide, has frequently been given misleading information about the adoptive family by a well-meaning caseworker to ensure her signature on the relinquishment paperwork. More fantasies are born.

In our modern society of true confessions, tell-all exposes, and acceptance of many levels of conduct previously considered taboo, it seems contradictory that society remains so close-minded concerning adoption. However, sealed records, which allow no access or exchange of identities between birth and adoptive parents, are still the most common legally practiced forms of adoption in this country. Without question, this system of closed records promotes secrecy or lies, and this is where fantasies are born. The unknown feeds our fantasies, creating desires, which encourage us to seek information and move toward reunion attempts.

A Tangled Web

According to the American Adoption Congress (AAC), nearly 3 percent of our population is adopted (*Decree*, 1998). This, in turn, translates to about 6 percent of the population of the United States being birth parents, given that it takes two to make a baby. Extending that to birth grandparents, both maternally and paternally, we must add about another 12 percent of the population, and that doesn't include siblings, aunts, uncles, and cousins. Try to imagine the numbers of people whose lives have been affected by adoption by remembering the old shampoo commercial: "You tell two friends, and they tell two friends, and they tell two friends, and so on, and so on. . . ." Whether they're aware of it or not, almost everyone in this country is either related to, or friends with, someone who is either adopted or has relinquished a child for adoption.

The sheer number of people whose lives are directly or indirectly affected by adoption would lead you to believe that the subject is a significant issue for social reform and civil rights activism within our society; in some circles, it *is* a significant issue for activism. But the majority of the public, who aren't adoption triad members and therefore haven't been directly affected by adoption, generally accept closed adoption records. Although some people genuinely believe that open adoption records create havoc within the family structure, most are simply ignorant about adoption issues, or led by blind faith in a system they view as traditional within adoption. Their apathy, or lack of knowledge about the issues, allows many lawmakers to support stricter laws concerning closed records, or at the least, to refuse legislation without protest or negative feedback from this unaffected populace.

Thankfully, efforts of activists, media attention, and a growing number of legislative champions, may make secrecy and closed records a thing of the past, at least when it comes to future adoptions. Laws are slowly changing across this nation. Reform and referendums like those recently witnessed in the states of Oregon, Tennessee, Delaware, and Alabama, as well as existing laws in Alaska and Kansas, provide adopted persons in those states access to their original birth records and/or adoption records.

States across this nation are beginning to recognize the rights of adult adoptees. They are finally creating methods for contact between consenting, biologically connected adults involved in adoption. States in support of registries, search assistance, intermediary programs, access to adoption records, or other options for reunion are on the rise. This is in despite of appeals and lobbying from organizations that support the closed records system, like the National Council for Adoption (NCFA) and the American Center for Law and Justice (ACLJ). These two groups have garnered the support of the religious right by erroneously claiming that birth mothers would rather have abortions than have the children they relinquish to adoption learn their identity. There is no reality base for these claims, as statistics from the two open record states, Kansas and Alaska, have proven. Adoption rates are up while abortion rates are down in these two states, and the four states that recently passed open records legislation should expect similar results over the next several years.

As we await the slow process of reform, we can certainly help the cause by supporting adoption organizations that lobby for open records. It is through these groups that reform has its best chance to flourish.

With continued influence and lobbying of highly recognized adoption rights organizations, such as the American Adoption Congress, Bastard Nation, Adoptees Liberty Movement Association, Concerned United Birthparents, Council for Equal Rights in Adoption, and others, open adoption records may be something we witness in our lifetime.

It is important to remember, however, that when records are opened, either independently or as the result of political reform, people will still have to make decisions as to how they plan to proceed with their newfound personal information. Many who seek and find biological family members are able to forge lasting relationships with the person for whom they were searching. Unfortunately, there are just as many searching folks who stumble through reunion feeling frustrated and disassociated, often terminating the relationship because the ignorance or insensitivity on one or the other's part became too overwhelming.

How to Use This Book

This book has been written to serve as a guide for biological family members either hoping for, or currently in, a reunion. It is not a step-by-step guidebook for you to follow literally. Some of the information might seem totally irrelevant to your specific case, whereas you may identify completely with other segments. You will read many personal anecdotes within these pages, included to provide you the opportunity to learn from other peoples' experiences— happy, as well as sad. In writing this book, our goal has been to equip you to make better decisions about the progression of your own reunion. At the end of some chapters, you'll find lists of questions that we hope will inspire you to start a journal detailing your emotional journey.

While we acknowledge that there are birth fathers deeply affected by relinquishment, the majority of them remain detached from the situation. With this in mind, in writing this book we have chosen to refer to the birth mother rather than the birth father in most instances. This is not intended to degrade or diminish those birth fathers who have been active participants and demonstrated their care and concern over having lost a child to adoption. We applaud those birth fathers who have shown support, remorse, or concern for their surrendered children. Our choice in language is simply an attempt to eliminate continual dual references, and is also based on AAC and other organizational information that shows that the majority of birth fathers are not participants in decisions concerning the relinquished child.

Regardless of what you absorb from these pages, one message will remain consistent throughout. Enter your reunion with caution, compassion, responsibility, and patience. If you exercise these four principles, then you will know you have entered your reunion honorably, regardless of its outcome.

May all of your reunion tears be tears of joy.

Part **1**

Preparing for a Reunion: What You Need to Know

Waves ripple
  Lovers cross
Sun rises
  Sand glistens
Nobody listens
  Mothers weep
Tears stain
  Labor delivers
Babies cry
  Youth dies
Ink dries
  Wonder why
Oh my
  Don't go
Didn't know
  Empty arms
Ache forever
  Heart grieves
Forgive me
  Didn't know
Didn't know
  Didn't know

—Julie Jarrell Bailey (1995)

Chapter 1

Understanding Your Fantasies and Feelings

The Reality Check

With the prospect of an adoption-based reunion comes time for a reality check. At some point in our adulthood—whether we're adopted or not—we each spend time reflecting upon and reviewing our life. We question decisions we made over the years and speculate on the variety of outcomes had we done something any other way than we actually did. Reflection is good for the soul. It gives us the opportunity to acknowledge mistakes, learn from them, and move on.

For the adopted person or birth mother, however, these times of reflection can lead to something other than moving on. Sometimes, we end up being stuck in the past, replaying scenarios over and over again with no conclusion or hope of closure. Some of us become prisoners of our past, serving life sentences with little hope for parole, waiting for a pardon to be issued by someone we've never met.

The Ghost Kingdom

Author Betty Jean Lifton (1994) describes a similar place in her book. She calls it the "Ghost Kingdom": "It is an awesome sphere, located only in the adoptee's psychic reality. The Forbidden Self, and occasionally even the Artificial Self, slips into the Ghost Kingdom to rendezvous with the lost mother and the lost baby, who never had a chance to grow into the child it should have been. The adoptee's fantasies, based as they are in the Ghost Kingdom, cannot connect with the outer world. They run the danger of becoming pathological when they interfere with the child's functioning in everyday life." (p. 57)

Lifton acknowledges, however, that fantasy also has a positive role when utilized as an escape from the "mysterious reality in which they find themselves, and as a way of holding on to some self-esteem." (p. 62)

Fantasies change over the years, too, as time passes and the infant grows into a toddler, a young child, a teenager, and then an adult. Each stage of development, as well as environmental influences, brings about new illusions, both in the one fantasizing and the one being fantasized about.

Fantasy vs. Reality

We should remember that fantasy is a healthy tool for the creative mind. As children, we are encouraged to use imagination in creating art, learning to read, visualizing math, and developing social skills. Fantasy is a basic part of the human psyche, and because it is based on imagination, which flows freely through our thought process, it can be fine-tuned with little effort on our part. Reality and fantasy have always coexisted. It's nothing new, and although the two ideas need little explanation, their blended states require a good deal of patience and understanding on our part as we use and observe them.

The advertising industry is a perfect example of how reality and fantasy can work together. It's simple: Words and images combine to stimulate our imaginations, blending our literal world with our personal desires.

The adoption Ghost Kingdom is not all that different from the world of advertising. It differs in the packaged product but not in the resulting satisfaction the viewer/visitor can achieve. Instead of dreaming of the perfect car or meal in the ad, adoption triad members may dream of driving that perfect car or eating that perfect meal with the one unidentified person to whom they have a biological connection.

A Child's Haven

Imagine that you are ten years old and one of your playmates, in anger, says something like, "Your real parents didn't even want you." This is a difficult moment in the life of an adopted child. Confusion sets in. He can acknowledge to himself that his friend is right. "Maybe she's right. Why else would I have been adopted?" But outwardly, it sets a feeling of defense in motion. He knows the people he calls "mom and dad" are not the parents to whom he was born—but they are the only parents he knows, and they are very real to him.

Scenes similar to this are familiar to the adopted person. Accusing an adopted child of not living with his "real parents" can create a deep emotional response, internally or externally. While he works his way through all of his conflicted emotions, he may enter and exit the Ghost Kingdom numerous times in the course of the day. He will revisit this place often throughout his lifetime, whenever conflict sets his defense emotions into action or he is simply looking for escape.

Adoptive parents may or may not be aware of the Ghost Kingdom fantasyland their child is experiencing. Even those parents who answer their adopted child honestly may not realize the world of dreams their child has entered. Regardless, a key signal of fantasizing that adoptive parents should recognize is when the child begins to ask questions about his birth family.

Make no mistake: The Ghost Kingdom can be a very healthy and safe place for the adopted child. He should spend time there as he works through personal issues and tries to stake a claim for his own identity. But he shouldn't live there and that is what adoptive parents need to monitor. The best way to help the child retain his own reality is by providing him with as much information about his birth family as possible.

Don't Ask, Don't Tell?

Until recent years, social workers discouraged adoptive parents from disclosing personal/biological information to the adoptee. It was believed that the less a child knew about her biological roots, the easier it would be for her to identify with her adoptive family and be accepted by her community. From the 1930s until very recent years, social workers and adoption agencies went to great lengths to match newborns with adoptive parents whose physical characteristics were most similar to the biological parents. The misconception that the adopted child would either be stigmatized or have difficulty bonding with her adoptive family was so great that many adoptive parents chose not to tell the child she was adopted.

Keeping Secrets

Angela noticed people pointing at her and whispering at family gatherings throughout her childhood and young adulthood. She vividly recalls a day on the playground when she was ten years old and a playmate accused her of not living with her "real parents."

Naturally, it evolved into other names being exchanged, and led to a scuffle. When Angela got home, she confronted her mother with the question: "Am I adopted?"

She remembers her mother breaking into hysteria and insisting that she had given birth to Angela. A few days later, her mother was hospitalized with what Angela calls "a nervous breakdown"—a situation that repeated itself over the years.

Angela's mother died when Angela was a young woman. When her father became bedridden with a terminal illness, he called her to his bedside and told her the truth about her birth. "I was forty- seven years old when I was finally told the truth about being adopted," Angela reflected with awe. "All of the whispering and finger-pointing when I was a kid was aimed at me. Everyone in my family knew I had been adopted except for me."

After Angela's father passed away, she discovered her adoption papers, which identified her birth parents. Her search was relatively easy, and within a matter of weeks, she had located her birth family. Sadly, both of her birth parents had passed away. Angela felt her search was successful, regardless, because it opened doors for her to meet not only her aunts and uncles, but also her half-siblings.

In hindsight, Angela realized she must have known on a sub-conscious level that she was adopted. She said, "I always felt very different from everyone in my family and my mother overreacted so severely whenever I asked questions."

Angela has no animosity toward her parents for keeping her birth status a secret. She continues to believe that they were victims of society as much as she was. Her only regret was not having her questions answered honestly and not knowing early enough to have had a reunion with her birth parents.

"Who Am I?"

Adopted or not, we all question our self-identity at times in our lives. Feelings of disassociation are commonplace during adolescence, as we strike out for independence and approach adulthood.

For the adopted person who has met his biological family, the feelings of disassociation dissipate over the years and closure coexists with the reality of family dynamics. However, for the adopted person not able to reunite with his birth parents, closure cannot completely exist, because there is no basis for the reality of family dynamics. The adopted person cannot assuredly identify the person from whom he received the green eyes, red hair, or proficiency in athletics, especially if he was raised in an adoptive family of brown-eyed brunettes who were literary geniuses and didn't know the difference between a touchdown and a jump-shot.

"I Am Different"

In his thought-provoking book, *Second Choice: Growing Up Adopted* (1993), Robert Andersen, M.D., offers insight from his perspective as an adoptee.

"What matters to me are the differences between adoptive and natural families and the consequences of these differences on the family members. More specifically, I care about what happens when these differences are unrecognized, ignored, or suppressed. The suppression caused me my biggest problems as an adoptee." (p. 31)

At an early age, Andersen recognized the ways he differed from his family. He was athletic and constantly in motion, while his parents worked on crossword puzzles and amateur radios. For many years, he perceived this inability to communicate and share interests as simply being an only child with no siblings with whom to interact. Andersen did not learn that he was adopted until he was twelve years old. Fuel was added to the flame of inner conflict when the Andersens were unable and/or unwilling to answer his questions truthfully and made statements that caused him to feel guilt and confusion over having asked anything about his adoption. Rather than be perceived as disloyal or unappreciative for what his family provided him, Andersen became submissive, only vocalizing his adoption questions to his closest friend.

"I dutifully renounced all interest in my biology, birth family, ancestry, heritage—in short, to a major part of my life—and no one questioned the absurdity of it all. I find that terribly disappointing. Are adoptees expected to take leave of their senses as well as their names?" (p. 38)

Not surprisingly, Andersen stopped asking questions about his adoption. It was another twenty years before he addressed the issues again. Tragically, Andersen learned that his adoption was what is called "black market," so for him, questions of his biology will probably remain unanswered forever.

For some adoptees, identity becomes a lifelong journey for answers to unanswerable questions. In much the same way, birth mothers search for reassurance and contentment regarding their surrendered child. Under the closed adoption system, both the adoptee and birth mother may never reach the destinations of their independent journeys. The adoptee might never know his heritage, and the birth mother might always question her decision about having relinquished her child for adoption. The unknown will always sit at the center of their universes.

"I Am Searching"

Doris, an adoptive mother, said of her now adult daughter, "She rarely asked any questions about her birth family, so I just presumed she really had no interest." Ironically, her daughter Monica, shared with her adoption support group that she was always afraid to ask too many questions about her birth family because she was afraid it would be interpreted as being disloyal to her adoptive family, or that they would think that she didn't love them.

"Curiosity about my birth family had nothing to do with the love I had for my adoptive family," Monica explained. "My adoptive family is my real family. I love them. But I always felt like I was part of a puzzle with a piece missing and I would never be able to complete the puzzle without having that one missing part."

Doris wanted to give Monica everything she wanted, including information about her birth family, but she wasn't able to pick up on the clues Monica occasionally dropped. Monica felt a deep loyalty to her adoptive family and was afraid they might abandon her if she asked too many questions about her birth family. Neither party was properly communicating with the other, and as years passed there were long periods where they didn't discuss these feelings at all.

As a teenager, Monica turned to substance abuse and sexual promiscuity as self-medication for the hurt she was unable to articulate. Her rebelliousness only served to increase the communication gap with her family. She said that she frequently imagined her birth family as being "absolutely perfect."

"I fantasized that they would be a stunningly beautiful couple who would pamper me and actually hear what I said instead of just patronizing me. They would spoil me with whatever I wanted and let me stay up late, watch whatever television shows or movies I wanted to see, eat what I wanted, whenever I wanted it, buy my own clothes—everything!" said Monica.

"In her early years, she was so eager to please everyone, but in her teenage years she acted like she just hated us all," Doris recalled.

Reflecting on her tumultuous teenage years, Monica now recognizes her role in the breakdown of communication with her family. She admits that in the beginning she was very eager to please her family. But she also remembers a time when she began noticing distinct differences between herself and her adoptive family. She convinced herself that she would not have the same kind of problems if she were with her biological family. Monica began spending more and more time fantasizing—living in her Ghost Kingdom—because that is where she got her questions answered and felt most comfortable with herself. As reality set in and the rift in her family relationship grew, she began to feel abandoned by the world. "I found comfort in drugs and booze because they made me numb to everything else around me," she said.

When Monica was seventeen years old, she became pregnant. She was afraid to tell her parents because she was convinced they wouldn't let her keep the baby, something she desperately wanted. Monica stopped taking drugs, and by the time the pregnancy had begun to show, she had significantly turned her life around. "I thought if I could just become that perfect little girl to my parents again, they would let me keep my baby," she rationalized.

Before she had a chance to tell them about her pregnancy, Monica's father died suddenly from a heart attack. His passing devastated the family financially, as well as emotionally. Monica said it was then that she realized she would not be able to raise her baby. She went to her mother with her news and together they made an adoption plan for the baby. Monica was ecstatic to have been allowed to select the couple who would parent her baby, and it gave her comfort to know that her son would have information about his birth parents.

However, within a few months following the relinquishment of her baby boy, Monica sank into a deep depression. Her mother attributed it to "postpartum blues," but Monica found her thoughts drifting to her fantasy world again, where she lived with her perfect family and no one had ever been abandoned or rejected. The reality of an open adoption for her own son while her records remained closed was overwhelming to Monica.

However, she didn't return to her old rebellious ways. Instead, Monica dove into her religion, hoping to pay penance for what she perceived to be her "sin." To the outside world, Monica appeared to be a spiritually happy young woman. Although contact with her son's adoptive parents diminished as a result of Monica's unresolved emotions, she did finish high school with honors and went to college. She finished college and got married, all the while harboring deeply buried feelings of inadequacy and low self-esteem. She began to experience a variety of health problems her doctors called "stress-related illness," which she couldn't understand because she didn't feel stressed.

It was another six years before a doctor diagnosed Monica with bipolar disorder (commonly called manic depression). With medication and therapy, Monica began to regain control of her emotions and her life. When her therapist suggested she join an adoption support group, Monica followed his advice. She credits the support group with restoring her will to live.

"It was the first time in my life that someone actually understood what I was feeling and didn't patronize me," she claimed. "I was able to review all of the events in my life when I had screwed up, and I understood some of the motives behind my actions. It was the first time I realized that I am the product of two families—one adopted and one biological—and that it wasn't disloyal of me to love them both."

Can Therapy Help?

As Monica's experience shows, dealing with psychological issues related to adoption can be a crucial step toward emotional health. However, as a whole, adoption issues are relatively new to the psychological profession. Even when adoptees inform their therapists of their adopted status, professionals often ignore that essential ingredient of the patient's emotional state and subsequent treatment. Psychologists frequently and mistakenly believe that adoption is not an issue; after all, the now-adult child was raised by his nonbiological family, and he has no real memories of his birth family. Therefore, any issues from childhood must be directly related to the family in which he was raised. What therapists may fail to realize is that regardless of upbringing, adoptees often experience conscious or subconscious feelings of abandonment and rejection by their birth mother. They don't perceive the consequences of the relinquishment and the need for closure as it relates to that loss.

Numerous support groups and adoption-related organizations have focused on educating professionals. Unfortunately, the process has been slow because many therapist are understandably resistant to change unless supported by adequate research, and statistical data on adoption issues is not abundant.

But times are changing, and as more adoption-based organizations collect their own data and present it for review to the psychology profession, more studies will be forthcoming. Only in recent years has the profession recognized that adoptees seek psychological intervention at a rate ten times greater than the nonadopted person, due to deeply rooted feelings of rejection and abandonment. While research on adoption issues continues to be slow, the recent discoveries have been influential in two ways: there's been a change in approach by many therapists when treating adopted patients, and an increasing number of colleges now offer courses in adoption as part of their curriculums.

Through education come understanding and solutions. The psychological profession changes constantly as new theories and research are brought to the forefront. There's now more hope for closure and ultimate healing for the adoptee and birth parent than in past years.

Taking the Next Step

Monica's quest for closure and emotional health wasn't over yet. Coming to terms with her own past was an awakening experience, but she still had many unanswered questions about her birth family. She had come so far and worked so hard that she felt emotionally ready to move on to the one thing that could possibly bring her closure to these disturbing issues: She decided to search for her birth mother.

The search took more than two years, but Monica and her birth mother, Maureen, finally had a tearful reunion. Monica's mother, Doris, remarked on the similar physical characteristics and gestures that Monica and Maureen share. "It's like seeing an aged reflection in the mirror," said Doris.

Monica's youthful fears that her adoptive family would feel she was disloyal and thus reject her turned out to be unfounded. In fact, the search and reunion process actually strengthened their relationship while providing vital genetic information for Monica—an observation noted in numerous case studies by authors Arthur Sorosky, M.D., Annette Baran, M.S.W., and Reuben Pannor, M.S.W., in their groundbreaking book, *The Adoption Triangle* (1978). The authors concluded that reunions most often strengthen the adoptive family relationship, because they dispel fears that the biological parent, once found, will somehow steal the child's love and affection for his adoptive family.

Through her search and reunion journey, Monica learned that she really has very little in common with her birth family and that none of the fantasies she ever had about them were even close to the truth. Regardless, she enjoys their relationship as friends, and they remain in contact.

Today, Monica is busy raising a family of her own, and she joyously introduced her children to their grandmothers—all of them. She is in touch with her relinquished son's adoptive parents in the best way for her, maintaining an appropriate distance but keeping the lines of communication open. The blending of her fantasies with the resulting realities of her life provided her the opportunity to expand her circle of love to members of both of her families—adoptive and biological.

What Can a Reunion Provide?

The realities of reunion are both complicated and simple. Reunion is often erroneously believed to be the simple reconnection of a relationship lost by the relinquishment and adoption process. While reunion admittedly provides a method of splicing those severed relationships, it also offers more for all three members of the adoption triad, depending on the level of reunion integration each is willing to accept.

For the birth mother or father, reunion can provide closure on many levels, particularly with issues over the past. Many birth parents hope to attain forgiveness for having relinquished their child, perceiving the reunion process as the opportunity to "right" an action that, in retrospect, they consider to have been "wrong." Reunion with the child sometimes provides both birth parents the opportunity to finally express themselves to each other, or simply about one another if they're not speaking, in a more open and honest manner than their youth and inexperience at the time of relinquishment allowed. This in itself can offer them a form of closure.

Let's not forget that birth mothers are in most ways no different than other "mothers" in our society. They are, for whatever given set of circumstances, unable to "parent," but are fully capable of being a "mother," coupled with all of the feelings and emotions we ascribe to that role. Reunion can give them a chance to express the overwhelming love that they feel.

Adoptees most often find reunion gratifying because it finally provides answers to questions they've had their entire lifetime. Many adoptees describe the experience of reunion as finally feeling in control of their destiny or at long last completing a partially painted picture. Regardless of the emotions involved, reunion definitely provides adoptees the chance to finally make their own choices in regards to their adoption—something they were unable to have a voice in when they were born.

Acknowledging Adoptive Parents

While adoptive parents seem to play the more silent role in the reunion process, either by their own choice or because the choice has been made for them by the adoptee, they have also spent many years in a Ghost Kingdom of their own. The difference is that most of their fantasies are based on fears of the unknown, particularly that the biological family will enter the picture and their child will shift his affections, abandoning the family who raised and nurtured him.

It is common for adoptive parents to feel overlooked as their child embraces his birth family. They may have to come to terms with suddenly being ignored during the decision-making process when historically, they were integral in every choice their child made. "I can't begin to describe how all of this reunion stuff makes me feel," one adoptive mother said. "My daughter calls her birth family frequently and she flies across the country for visits that I only learn about after the fact. I know it sounds trite to say that my feelings are hurt over all of this, but I don't know how else to describe it. It really goes deeper than just hurt feelings. I was so supportive of her finding her birth family, but nothing prepared me for this kind of treatment."

There are few words of comfort to offer adoptive parents when their adult child in reunion seems to shut them out of the reunion process. Adoptive parents may experience feelings of abandonment by their child, but as everyone settles into reunion, the feelings, fears, and fantasies disperse as the adoptee and birth family move past their "honeymoon" phase of reunion.

It's important, however, that adoptive parents give their grown child the temporary distance they need to embrace reunion. It might help adoptive parents to relate the importance of a reunion in its early stages to some other life event fraught with emotion, like a wedding. Weddings bring out both the best and the worst in the bride and groom, as well as everyone involved in the planning process. A high level of anxiety exists for everyone as they work to accommodate the masses, knowing in the end that someone isn't going to be 100 percent satisfied.

Reunion, like a wedding, must go through its own natural, progressive stages all the way through the first year of life together. It takes at least that long, sometimes longer, for everyone involved to reach a level of comfort and healing from all that evolved before the "big day."

It's also important to acknowledge that adoptive parents benefit from adoption reunions as well. It allows them to have answers regarding their child's social/medical history. It also acknowledges on a much deeper level that love is neither bought nor sold, but nurtured, and the foundation of love their family unit was built on is not shaken by a reunion.

At a legislative hearing in 1998, an adoptive mother expressed her views on open records with amazing compassion: "As a society, we have no problem accepting the fact that a mother can love more than one child. But we seem to have a real problem allowing our children to love more than one mother. Frankly, I welcome as many people into my child's life as will love them, and this includes their birth family."

Her insight summarizes the true essence of the journey.

Don't Play Their Game

Understandably, all three adoption triad members will have different preconceived notions about reunion, many of which are shaped by the media. Hollywood producers have made billions of dollars playing on our worst nightmares, including adoption scenarios. But if it weren't for inaccuracies, embellishments, and exploitation by the media and movie industries, our imaginations regarding the subject of reunion might not be so vivid. Don't allow made-for-TV movies, television talk shows, news features or other media stories about reunion influence you. Your reunion won't be anything like the ones you see on television or read about in magazines and newspapers. Yours will be uniquely your own, guided by your own personality and comfort level, not by a paid producer.

While your associates outside the adoption triad may have little understanding of or sensitivity to your dreams, your emotions surrounding reunion must be validated. Embrace your feelings and don't make apologies to anyone. It's impossible for someone who has not lived your life to comprehend the emotions you feel or the fantasies you imagine, so don't allow other people to invade your emotional space.

A Tale of Two Adoptees

Jenny's adoptive mother insisted that she get involved with a local adoption search and support group. She explained that Jenny had always had identity issues and had built up many fantasies about her birth parents, which had caused her a number of psychological problems over the years.

Jenny was a young woman, approaching age thirty, who continued to act out aggressively whenever she felt she was being denied something she desired. Her therapist theorized that Jenny had channeled much of her frustration regarding her closed adoption records into a rage disorder that at times was explosive. Although medication helped Jenny control her disorder, she was compelled to continue searching for her birth mother.

After an eight-year search, she found her birth mother, who had coincidentally been searching for Jenny, also. Unfortunately, it was too late. Jenny's birth mother had lost her fight against a terminal illness several year earlier, so their introduction took place at the graveside.

Jenny blamed the closed records system for keeping her from her birth mother while the opportunity existed. She believed a reunion was their right, especially since they were both consenting adults. The agency had copies of both their letters on file, but the legal system prevented them from sharing any information with the other, despite her birth mother's illness.

"I hate them all and just wish I could go blow up their building," Jenny would say about the adoption agency and vital statistics department in her state. While her aggression apparently still exists, Jenny is grateful that her search provided her a reunion with her half-siblings, as well as with her biological father—all of whom have become vital interests in her life.

Norman, on the other hand, adopted as an infant, felt that any contact with his birth family was intrusive—an invasion of his privacy. "I love my adoptive parents. They are my real parents and I don't need anyone else," he said.

Norman lived in a foster home until he was nearly a year old before being adopted by his current family. Although he finally became attached to his adoptive family, he didn't feel secure with them until he reached school age. Even today, Norman admits that he has always mistrusted relationships—no one has been able to live up to his expectations—nor has he been able to sustain lengthy friendships. He refers to his adoptive mother as his "best friend," and he's emotionally attached to her, as well as to his adoptive father. "I would never want to do anything that might hurt her or my dad. They've given me a life I would never have had if I had been raised by my birth family."

In his support group, Norman confessed that he might be more interested in a relationship with his birth family after both of his adoptive parents have died. For now, however, he doesn't want to "upset the apple cart."

Norman's emotions are commonplace among adoptees. Many are torn between issues of loyalty and desire for knowledge. Many adoptees choose to wait until after their adoptive parents die before searching for their biological family. Unfortunately, waiting brings the added risk that they will find their birth parents also in the grave, which can bring on an entirely new set of complicated emotional (as well as identity) issues. But this same loyalty can also help the searching adoptee approach reunion very responsibly, because they are already sensitive to issues of intrusion and privacy.

The experiences of those who have had reunions makes one thing clear: No one experiences the reunion that they fantasized about. Some are better than any preconceived notions, while others are tragic disappointments. Regardless of their experiences, however, the vast majority of adoptees and birth parents we've talked to agree that they would repeat their search process because finding the information they had sought for so many years was satisfying.

Beyond Fantasy: Coming to Terms with Your Identity

Many emotional issues can surface for the adoptee as he moves through his personal Ghost Kingdom and into the reality of his identity. Healing work is vital. A primary realization for the adopted person is that he's the product of two families—not just the biological family or the adoptive family, but both. This acknowledgment can offer healing in its simple recognition. To recognize the roles both families have had on the adopted person's life also helps him to more clearly establish his identify and understand his own complexities.

Francie Portnoy, M.A., psychotherapist and author of *One Wonderful You* (1997), is also an adoptee. When she wrote about her life experiences as an adoptee for the magazine *Adoptive Families of America* (1998), she provided other adoptees insight into methods of working to heal their own issues of grief and loss, while also helping them come to terms with their own identities. A portion of her article, "Two Family Legacies," is reprinted below with the author's permission.

Two Family Legacies

Who is this kid? All parents, at one time or another, ask this question. I am most likely to ask it, accompanied by a sigh, when one of my kids is acting up. Who is this kid? Where did she get that behavior? Often, though, the behavior in question is part of me—a part I really don't wish to acknowledge, but, when I am honest with myself, is as familiar as the face in the mirror. Most of the time the behaviors of my children, both positive and negative, are recognizable. They belong to either their father or me.

This, I know, was not always the case for my parents. I was not a familiar image to them. Not only was I physically different from most of the family, being skinny and blond in a family of dark-haired, zaftig (translate as Rubenesque) women, but my personality was, at times, alien to them. Although both my sister and I were adopted at infancy, my looks and personality were more dissimilar to the family than hers were. Growing up, most of the children in our extended family were compliant, as was my sister. I, however, tested most of the limits. Even within our adoptive family, both of us children were unique.

Science determined many years ago that genetics play a major role in our health and physical appearance. It has also been proven that many medical conditions, as well as the potential range of intellectual ability, are also genetically linked. But it has only been within the past few decades that we are finally understanding its depths in relation to our personality, talents, and gender, as well as social preferences.

Some of the most interesting studies on this question have come out of the University of Minnesota (1999). Since the late 1970s, when Thomas Bouchard began his work in this area of research, the university has been studying identical twins reared apart since infancy in order to determine the influence both genetics and environment have on the individual. The research has shown that twins reared apart were about 50 percent similar in personality traits and that these similarities in personality were due to genetics. Since identical twins have the same genetic makeup, it was further concluded that the differences in the personalities of the twins reared apart were due to their environments. In other words, statistically speaking, about half of a child's personality can be attributed to genetics, and half to environment. Looking at each individual child though, the range of contribution of genes and environment will vary— one child being more strongly influenced by genetics, another by environment.

So, if the influence of genes and environment is a fifty-fifty ratio and the children in both biological families and adoptive families are often unique, why is this issue important to adoptive parents? Why should they bother spending any energy looking at the nature versus nurture issue?

Although being in a biological family doesn't guarantee that a child will be similar to other family members, it does increase her chances greatly. Even if she is not a mirror image of her parents, there is usually some other person in the family with whom she can identify. In adoptive families, however, where there are similarities, the child eventually understands that this is by coincidence, not because of any biological connection.

Knowing there is a common bond—physically, emotionally, or preferentially—with another human being is important to many adopted children. Although it helps to have some concrete knowledge about your child's birth family in order to help her feel this sense of genealogical connectedness, it is not always necessary. Understanding what traits your child has that did not come from your family (physical are most obvious, but consider personality, abilities, and preferences) can give you a lot of information that will help your child feel a sense of connectedness to her past while empowering her as a unique individual.

This integrating of the birth family legacy into an adopted child's identity is a process, not a one-time event. This integration will take place at various times during your child's development and in different ways, often coinciding with each developmental stage. You might start out talking about the existence of the birth family, then move on to comparing and contrasting physical characteristics, and as your child is able to understand that less concrete traits like personality, abilities, and preferences are affected by genetics, broaden your discussions to include them. This brings us to something even more important than knowing about the genetic and environmental contributions to your child. More important than nature or nurture is the interplay between the two—how the nurture, your legacy to your child as adoptive parents, supports nature, the legacy of the birth family.

Even before your child becomes part of your family, your history is beginning to influence your relationship with her. As each of us is growing up, we imagine our futures by playing them out in our heads. Our individual family histories and social interactions greatly influence our ideas about our perfect future and fantasy family, since what we value about ourselves and others is greatly influenced by what our families and significant others valued about us. This picture of a family that you have carried with you since childhood will be used to measure and judge your reality family. It will be part of the family legacy you pass on to your child—a legacy that will most likely include some great stuff as well as some expectations that may be impossible for your child to meet.

If you are not conscious of your fantasies about your life and your family, they could affect your reality family, including your real child, in negative ways. No child is perfect, and if your child has to measure up to your fantasy child, she will most likely fall short.

Understanding your fantasy family and the fact that your child is greatly influenced by another family's genetic legacy will assist you in honoring your child as the unique person she is. Because even more important than what makes your child who she is, is how she feels about who she is—her self-esteem.

You may, at times, still ask, "Who is this kid?" All parents do. But when your child looks in the mirror, she will not have to ask, "Who am I?", for she will know that she is a unique blend of two family legacies. She will know that the person she has become is a direct result of adoption. When she looks in the mirror, she may not see your face smiling back at her, but she will like the face she sees. And that is what healthy parenting is all about.

Questions to Contemplate: Are You Ready to Move Toward Reunion?

Begin your journal with some basic questions about what you expect and what you need to do to prepare.

For Birth Parents:
It is true that many birth parents cannot fully work through the loss of a child, particularly since closed adoption represents a lack of closure. Recognizing this, you can prepare yourself mentally and examine the realities of the adoption. Your child is no longer "your child" by virtue of association. Your child has parents, and this actuality must be accepted before you proceed toward reunion. Ask yourself:

- How do I define adoption reunion and what is it I really seek from reunion?

- Do I believe my relinquished child will become "my child" in reality?

- Am I prepared to provide only information without a personal relationship if that's all my child desires?

- Have I acquainted myself with information pertaining to current adoption issues?

For Adoptees:
Remember that your birth family did in certain senses probably go on with their lives. There will be other family members to consider: spouses, children, grandparents. Ask yourself:

- How do I define "adoption reunion" and what do I hope to achieve by having one?

- Am I seeking a family in reunion?

- Am I seeking just information (medical, social, etc.)?

- What do I see as my responsibilities for opening a door into the lives of other people?

Chapter **2**

Exploring Family Bonds and the Trauma of Separation

Adoption is an enigma, a growing paradox with each generation. On one level, adoption is viewed as the ultimate sacrifice on the part of a birth mother. Internet chat folders on adoption issues are filled with comments from adoptive parents and others who sing the praises of the selfless birth mother who found the inner strength and courage to relinquish her child to the sanctified institution of adoption. Yet, on another level, birth mothers are severely scrutinized and subjected to such intimidating questions as, "How could you have given away your own flesh and blood?" and "What kind of woman are you?" They may also face judgmental statements putting their morality in question.

Perhaps the most significant contradiction comes from our own society. Social service departments across the country agree that, except in cases of abuse or neglect, the first choice and best situation for any child is to remain with his biological family. However, when a single mother chooses to parent, society stigmatizes her with unkind names and inadequate (albeit vital) social welfare programs.

Paradox in Relinquishment

"R.W.," a birth mother featured in the book *Faces of Adoption* (Giddens 1983), summarized a social bias that still affects some unmarried pregnant women, two decades later: "We are told how saintly we are to give our child a better life, then called whores and prostitutes for doing so." (p. 32)

Although attitudes have changed somewhat, the birth mother may still feel she is being punished by society for being caught, literally, with her pants down. To complicate the situation, family members often refuse financial and emotional support, and the boyfriend who once made faithful promises may quickly disappear after hearing the news of pregnancy.

Once all support and hope is yanked from the birth mother, society insists that the birth mother "made her own choice" when she decided to relinquish her child for adoption. We fail to see our own role in the coercion of the relinquishment.

Well-meaning social workers, parents, and friends often encourage the unwed pregnant woman to surrender the baby for adoption "in the best interest of the child," emphasizing the girl's shortcomings and inability to financially support the baby. The young birth mother finds herself torn between her love for the child she has carried for nine months and the realization that, without help, she won't be adequately prepared to provide anything more than love for the baby.

In the end, when her feelings of hopelessness eat away her self-confidence, she signs the papers. Sometimes, these are tear-filled moments. Other times the young woman hides behind a stoic face, afraid to let anyone see her fear and disappointment in herself. Very few of the birth mothers we've talked to willingly relinquished their children, and those that do tend to have extenuating circumstances that were factors to ease the decision-making process, such as rape, serious illness, safety issues, or physical limitations.

Birth mothers who relinquish are told to put this moment in time behind them, to forget it, to move on with their lives. They are reminded that they will have other children in the future, when they are married and ready to be a parent. While these words of wisdom are meant to be reassuring, and some birth mothers attempt to follow the advice, they are not words based on a birth mother's reality. Birth mothers may move on with their physical lives, but they do not ever forget the child they relinquished.

The Long-term Effect of Relinquishment

E. Lynn Giddens, coauthor of this book, made an interesting discovery while researching her thesis, *Post-Traumatic Stress Disorder Symptoms in Birth Mothers* (1998). She learned that contrary to popular belief, a birth mother doesn't forget the child she surrendered to adoption, nor does the passage of time necessarily mean that she is able to "move on with her life," as previously claimed by adoption workers.

An interesting aspect Giddens noted was that a birth mother's degree of emotional trauma varied depending on whether or not she had experienced a reunion or was still searching for her child. She concluded that a high percentage of birth mothers experience post-traumatic stress disorder (PTSD) due to relinquishment and possibly genetic factors as well. However, birth mothers who were victims of a closed adoption record system and had no knowledge about their child continued to suffer more significantly than birth mothers who had experienced either open adoptions or reunion. Comments from birth mothers included the following:

- "I had no idea I would feel so much pain, and I don't mean just the physical stuff with labor and delivery. I'm talking about the emotional pain of having lost a part of myself. That part will stay with me forever."

- "They told me that I would forget it all over time. They lied. I haven't forgotten anything—especially the emptiness I feel without my baby."

- "I'll always remember talking and singing to my baby boy while he practiced karate in my tummy. It was the best and worst time of my life."

- "Food tasted so weird while I was pregnant. Breyer's Mint Chocolate Chip Ice Cream was the only thing that satisfied my taste buds, so I ate it just about every day. Today, it gags me just to smell it. The really funny part is that when I found my daughter and we were comparing similarities, she told me that Breyer's Mint Chocolate Chip Ice Cream was her favorite food!"

- "Even though I knew I couldn't keep him, I really loved feeling him move inside my belly. It made me feel secure about everything. But it all came crashing in after he was born and they took him away, forever."

- "I just want to know if she's had a happy life. Then I'll know for sure if I did the right thing for her."

Bonding and Wounding

In her book, *The Primal Wound* (1993), Nancy Newton Verrier discusses the subject of in utero bonding at great length. Verrier, a psychotherapist as well as an adoptive mother, made some interesting discoveries. In addition to her own experiences, Verrier offers insight based on the work of such notable professionals as Dr. T. Berry Brazelton, Dr. David Chamberlain, Donald Winnicott, and Judith Viorst, all of whom agree on one level or another that mother-and-child bonding begins in the womb.

Verrier writes, "Many doctors and psychologists now understand that bonding doesn't begin at birth, but is a continuum of physiological, psychological, and spiritual events which begin in utero and continue throughout the postnatal bonding period. When this natural evolution is interrupted by a postnatal separation from the biological mother, the resultant experience of abandonment and loss is indelibly imprinted upon the unconscious minds of these children, causing that which I call the 'primal wound.'" (p. 1)

A significant portion of society must agree that in-utero bonding occurs between mother and child, because many people continue to question the woman who relinquishes, wondering how she could surrender to strangers a life she carried for nine months. It is clear that separation of parent and child can have a devastating effect on both persons, regardless of whether or not the devastation is publicly displayed. While adoption provides a sound solution to a crisis and may ultimately be the best choice for all involved, we must remember that all three members of the adoption triad feel a loss, and we must be sensitive in an attempt to help them heal the wounds.

"Loss is paramount in the understanding of what is going on with each member of the adoption triad," Verrier explained. "The adoptee is feeling the loss of the birth mother, the birth mother is feeling the loss of her child, and the adoptive parents are feeling loss of their fertility and genetic continuity. None is able to grieve, sometimes because the feelings are so repressed or denied as to make them inaccessible; other times because society ignores their grief and thinks that the adoptee and adoptive parents should feel lucky, and that the birth mother made her choice and should get on with her life." (p. 109)

Secondary Wounding

In her book *I Can't Get Over It: A Handbook for Trauma Survivors* (1996), Dr. Aphrodite Matsakis discusses a type of trauma that she calls, "secondary wounding." Although this book on post-traumatic stress disorder (PTSD) was written primarily for victims of violent crimes and sexual abuse, Dr. Matsakis's theory of secondary wounding accurately portrays trauma resulting from the adoption process.

"As important to the healing process as other people are, it's an unfortunate truth that often people do more harm than good. Strangers who don't understand your situation can be unintentionally cruel, but so can those who should know better: family, friends, and helping professionals. Instead of being supported, you may have been made to feel ashamed of having been a part of a traumatic event in the first place, of your reactions to the event or symptoms you have developed as a result, or even of asking for help.

"Secondary wounding occurs when the people, institutions, caregivers, and others to whom the trauma survivor turns for emotional, legal, financial, medical, or other assistance respond in one of the following ways. . . ." (p. 90)

In summary, Dr. Matsakis concludes that secondary wounding occurs when others:

- Disbelieve, deny, or discount the trauma, or minimize the magnitude of the event and its meaning to the victim, or its impact on the victim's life;

- Blame the victim, increasing her sense of self-blame and low self-esteem;

- Stigmatize by judging the victim negatively via ridicule, condescension, misinterpretation, punishment, or implication; or

- Deny assistance.

All of Dr. Matsakis's theories on secondary wounding are applicable to both the birth mother and the adoptee:

- Society contributes to the birth mother's low self-esteem with statements such as, "What kind of woman would give up her own flesh and blood?" These comments support the idea that she deserves whatever negative treatment she experiences and can be very stigmatizing.

- Adoptees are discounted and denied support when they seek a reunion with their biological family by being made to feel that they do not appreciate their adoptive family or are being disloyal by asking questions.

- Birth mothers are discounted when they are told, "You made your choice, now live with it," despite the lack of support that leads to the "choice" to relinquish.

- Adoptees who seek knowledge about themselves often face blaming, guilt-inducing comments such as, "You couldn't have asked for a better family than you were raised in," or "You should appreciate what you already have and not go looking for something that might not exist."

- Birth mothers are stigmatized with labels such as "slut," "whore," "tramp," and "low-class," resulting in a fear of telling anyone about their relinquishment, as well as low self-esteem.

- Adoptees are stigmatized with labels such as "bastard," "illegitimate," "ungrateful," and "bad blood."

Dr. Matsakis summarizes the cause of secondary wounding on a level to which both birth mother and adoptee can surely relate: "In essence, secondary wounding occurs because people who have never been hurt sometimes have difficulty understanding and being patient with people who have been hurt." (p. 93)

If, in essence, secondary wounding stems primarily from ignorance and cultural/societal influences as Dr. Matsakis theorizes, then secondary wounding must play a major role in the PTSD effects of adoption, as most of the population is inexperienced in the emotional trauma adoption triad members experience.

Lasting Imprints

When a newborn child is handed to strangers, that loss is imprinted permanently within the baby, as well as within the psyche of the birth mother. It may be years before the child or birth mother is able to articulate the submerged feelings related to the separation. In fact, they may never be able to articulate the experience, but one way or another, they will act out their feelings in an attempt at expression.

The research of many professionals supports the belief that a birth mother's state of mind can effect hormonal changes that contribute to the unborn child's emotional and physical health. For example, if a birth mother actively participates in making the adoption plan, such as meeting the adoptive parents and formulating openness in the adoption, she internalizes less stress herself, which is ultimately less stressful on the fetus. In open adoptions of today, many adoptive parents participate in the birthing process of their child. They are actually in the delivery room to begin the bonding process immediately following birth.

Regardless of well-intended actions that minimize stress levels for all three adoption-triad members, the newborn will still sense separation from his birth mother. Studies by many eminent professionals, including Dr. David Chamberlain (1988), conclude that newborn babies are cognitive beings and able to recognize their birth mothers. If babies are able to recognize their birth mothers, then they should certainly recognize when they have been separated.

Bonding between mother and child is unquestionably unique. The bond created at birth creates a lifeline for the child, a genealogy and general feeling of being connected to something greater than he is. While adoption can provide him with a strong support network and a loving and nurturing environment, it may always lack something on the level of self-completion.

Questions to Contemplate:
The Reality of Entering a Person's Life

Entering another person's life is a major undertaking that requires serious consideration. These questions will help you understand where you're starting from and where you'd like to end up. Ask yourself:

For Birth Parents:

- Have I worked through any feelings I might have toward the adoptive parents?

- Am I willing to open the door in my life despite whatever condition my relinquished child might be in?

- Are there unspoken obligations when I make the choice of entering someone's life? If so, what are they?

- What have I imagined my role to be in relation to the adoptee? Their mother? Their birth mother? Their friend?

- Am I emotionally prepared to accept the adoptive parents, siblings, extended family members, friends?

- What if I'm not allowed to enter the life of the adoptee or their adoptive family? How will I react?

For Adoptees:

- Am I prepared, once entering the search/reunion process, to be mindful of the other person's feelings?

- Am I prepared to be accepted or rejected by my birth sibling?

- If the birth parent is married, am I prepared for spousal acceptance or rejection?

- What obligations do I foresee when I enter this other family unit's world?

Chapter **3**

Coping with Loss and Other Emotions

The uniting truth about adoption is the fact that it always involves loss. For the adoptive parent who has never had children, it is often the loss of their own fertility and therefore their ability to carry on their genetic lineage. One or both of the adoptive parents often feel like they have failed the other one by not being able to have children.

The birth mother feels the loss of a life she carried for nine months. She grieves much the same way as the mother who has lost her child to illness, accident, or other tragedy, only she is not able to acknowledge her grief publicly, so she internalizes. Birth mothers frequently lose their self-esteem after relinquishment.

The adoptee has lost all choice in the process, and, most importantly, the vitality of a biological connection. Unfortunately, adoptees in our society remain children in the eyes of the law, regardless of their age. Most states in this country maintain sealed adoption records, so when an adult adoptee makes a grown-up choice to learn more about his biological family, he continues to be treated as a child and is denied access to his own personal, vital information.

In Verrier's insightful book, discussed in the previous chapter, she describes the profundity of loss. Recognizing that loss is not very well understood in our society, she points out that even on joyous occasions, loss can exist. A primary problem in our society is our lack of sensitivity regarding the impact loss plays in life. Unexpressed grief from loss often remains repressed for years, only to play out physically or psychologically, in the form of stomachaches, headaches, stress, withdrawal, and depression.

The Inability to Share in Loss

Julie Jarrell Bailey shares the story of how she came to understand loss:

As a writer, I am often accused by my friends of having an edge over them when it comes to expressing emotions. That may be true of me today (all speculative, of course), but it hasn't always been my good fortune. There have been times in my life when words were utterly lost to me. My emotions remained intact, but I had no voice—at least no voice to adequately express the emotions I experienced.

I am one of seven children. When I was thirteen years old, my oldest brother, Stephen, then eighteen years old, died tragically in an automobile accident. My mother mourned his loss for years, haunted by nightmares. I recall seeing her lying in bed, searching for solace, staring at Steve's lone portrait on the wall. She was devastated by his death, as were we all, and she returned to his grave frequently, not realizing she had withdrawn from friends and family. Even after we moved to another state, mother would order flowers to be placed on his grave and visited his burial site each time she drove north.

I spent most of my teenage life observing my mother's grief and emotional distance. I felt guilty for being one of the survivors, although I was not involved in the accident. When Stephen died, I overheard someone comment to my mother, "Well, Mrs. Jarrell, at least you have six more children at home." My mother responded, "That's no consolation, I promise you."

My interpretation of this comment, combined with the emotional barriers my grief-stricken mother had erected, set a pattern of emotional distance from my mother that lasted for many years. I translated the words, "That's no consolation, I promise you," as "I could never love any of the remaining six children as much as I loved Steve." That misinterpretation provided me with an excuse to treat my mother in ways that I only pray my children never treat me.

Of course, my realization today, as a middle-aged adult with children of my own, is that my mother had actually just corrected the well-intentioned acquaintance. In short, Mom had told the woman that all of us were equally loved, and that one child cannot replace another in a mother's heart because each is a treasure in its own right.

Back in 1973, when I was barely nineteen years old and

relinquished my daughter for adoption, I felt as though my baby had died. My heart ached to hold her in my arms, but they remained empty despite my cries—cries exactly like I heard my mother make from behind closed doors when Stephen died. The difference was that there was no grave for me to visit and no photos to cry over, and I had been told to keep my daughter's birth and relinquishment a secret so people wouldn't judge me harshly. Frankly, even if I had possessed a photograph of my baby, there could have been no consolation. She was gone from my life, supposedly forever, and under the closed adoption system, I was never allowed to know anything else about her.

Despite both of us having lost our firstborn children, my mother was unable to comfort me in my loss. When I finally began the search for my daughter nearly twenty years later, I realized the irony we shared.

In retrospect, I don't believe it was because mother didn't want to console me. I believe it was because she simply didn't know how to approach me. She was the product of a generation where secrets were easily accepted and affection was difficult to demonstrate. Added was the fact that teenagers, by nature, have a knack for creating distance between themselves and their parents through normal growth and development. And our relationship had a few additional elements contributing to the chasm.

She wasn't able to gauge the depth of my loss because I wouldn't allow her in. I was hurt over having lost my daughter. I was angry that my parents didn't perceive my hurt and didn't offer to help me keep my baby. I felt they should have known that I was in misery from my loss without me having to say something. But adoption issues weren't discussed in 1973, and the correlation between relinquishment and grief had not yet been made.

For many years my loss translated to an emotional distance between me and my mother, as well as my father. I suffered from numerous health problems because of my unresolved grief, and I was haunted by recurring nightmares about the daughter I had lost. I didn't know how to cope—worse, I didn't believe that I could cope with the grief I had suppressed. The loss of my daughter and the emotions I had attached to the relinquishment were never discussed. I lied to myself and to everyone else about the loss I suffered for many years. Sadly, most of the birth mothers I've met over the past ten years suffered in much the same way. Suffering in silence seems to be the unifying bond of birth mothers, just as suffering with unanswerable questions unites adoptees.

Stages of Grief

In her groundbreaking book *On Death And Dying* (1968), Dr. Elisabeth Kubler-Ross discussed the varying stages of grief and the anticipated behaviors expected of someone suffering from loss. While working with terminally ill patients and their families, she had observed certain patterns of emotion, which she identified as the five stages of grief. The stages are listed here, along with some of the associated behaviors, which may help you to identify the stages within yourself:

- Anger—protest, rage

- Depression—withdrawal, crying

- Denial—disbelief, distrust

- Bargaining—superficial promises, a little give-and-take

- Acceptance—the point when life doesn't look so terrible and you're able to resume your old lifestyle from a better emotional perspective

These stages of grief can be applied to the losses experienced by all triad members. The newborn removed from his birth mother will cry incessantly, despite the comfort of his surroundings. Likewise, many a birth mother has been described as "having a chip on her shoulder" following relinquishment, which is another form of anger.

Even adoptive parents—who are perceived to gain the most in adoption—experience grief before, during, and after the legal process is completed. Excluding adoptive parents who adopt for reasons other than infertility, imagine the stages of grief infertile couples experience when they first learn of their inability to reproduce. Would you be angry first, or jump immediately to acceptance? The interesting thing about the stages of grief is how you can jump from one point to another and back again, at any time, without having to follow any sequence.

There's another type of grief adoptive parents experience. Imagine yourself as a cute, cuddly newborn baby. Your birth mother has left you at the hospital after signing relinquishment papers. You've spent nine months inside her womb, so you know who your "familiar" is, but suddenly, she's not around. Your comfort zone is compromised. You are so upset that your mother isn't answering your cries, day after day.

One day a nice couple walks in and takes you to your new home. It's not where your familiar mother is. This is a new place. Just as your new parents pick you up to snuggle, coo, and feed you, your rage takes over. You cry like someone has scalded you with boiling water, despite all of the love surrounding you. Nothing your adoptive mother does comforts you. Do you think her realization that she's unable to comfort you might cause her some grief? You bet it does. Only time and consistent reassurance that she's staying with you can improve the situation.

With very little imagination, you can probably identify behaviors in your own life that might compare to the stages of grief as they apply to adoption. Loss is a tragedy on all levels—and if you don't allow yourself time to grieve, your loss might haunt you forever.

Resolution in Grief

Psychology professionals today believe there may be many more stages than the initial five identified by Kubler-Ross, but most agree that these five stages include all the emotions experienced by the grieving person.

As a society, we don't deal very well with issues of grief. We seem to be uncomfortable with the subject. We tend to shy away from grieving people, or, quite the opposite, pamper them—neither of which is beneficial to the suffering person.

Replacing What We've Lost

Because of our discomfort with the mourning process, we often look for ways to quickly replace what we've lost. If our cat dies, we might drive down to the animal shelter and get a new kitten. If our job is suddenly terminated, we quickly send out résumés or contact a headhunter. If a loved one dies, we might bury ourselves with our work or recreation or family—anything to divert our attention from what we have lost.

In adoption, a common view perpetuated by well-meaning social workers, friends, and family members is that the birth mother can have other children, insinuating that she can replace the child she has lost. This myth grows from a desire to comfort the young birth mother, and due to her inexperience in the adult world, she often believes whatever she is told. In actuality, many birth mothers are never again able to have children. While researching their groundbreaking book, *The Adoption Triangle* (1978), Sorosky, Baran, and Pannor discovered that about 40 percent of the birth mothers in their sample experienced secondary infertility. At the National Adoption Awareness Convention in 1995, Pannor disclosed that the figures today have grown significantly, and he believes that as much as 60 percent of the birth mother population is affected by infertility problems. Admittedly, these statistics are not definitive, but their discovery opens many questions and clearly identifies the need for further research in this area.

Regardless, this secondary form of infertility is an entirely new form of loss and raises additional questions related to closed adoption records. Is there a moral imperative that a birth mother with secondary infertility be allowed to contact the child whom she surrendered to another family?

Disruption: A Rarely Discussed Loss

Disruption is what takes place when an adoption doesn't work out. Essentially, it is adoption in reverse. Though it's rarely discussed, disruption is a reality in some adoptions—and it results in another type of loss. At a 1996 workshop in Chapel Hill, North Carolina, a state employee revealed that up to 10 percent of all adoptions end in disruption for a variety of reasons:

- The adoptee has unmanageable behavioral disorders or other disorders for which the adoptive family is unprepared.

- The adoptee requests removal from the adoptive home.

- The court declares the adoption invalid or "wrongful." This would include cases of fraud on the part of the adoption agency, misrepresentation of the adoptive parents, and falsification or inaccurate disclosure of serious information about the adoptee that might have influenced the adoptive parents prior to adoption.

- The youth is emancipated before age eighteen.

- Other realities of life intrude, of the type that affect many families: death, divorce, or mental illness; abuse, neglect, or other criminal action. Disruption doesn't automatically occur with one of these events, but an occurrence lays the groundwork for a possible disruption.

- The match between adoptee and adoptive parents was not good; as with bad marriages, sometimes personalities just don't mesh.

Disruption is never the goal of an adoption. For an adopted child to be removed from the home of his adoptive parents, some very serious events must have occurred. Nevertheless, some adoptions do not last forever.

How does this affect reunion? Will the adoptee be angry and reject the birth parent who searches? Will the birth mother or father be so guilt-ridden that they are unable to face and sustain a reunion with their biological child? The answers cannot be predicted here because everything is dependent upon the individual people and their ability to forgive, as well as their ability to offer and receive unconditional love.

It is highly possible that despite disruption, the birth parent–adoptee relationship can be as successful as any other reunion. The dynamics of the issues may seem greater than the traditional adoption-based reunion due to the added trauma, but a successful reunion can be achieved, regardless of circumstance. While it is important for both parties to exercise compassion and caution as they tread the course of reunion, it is imperative that the adoptee and birth parent work together to heal the wounds caused by both the relinquishment and subsequent disruption.

A professional therapist and/or an adoption support group can be helpful in this situation. Support is important throughout the healing process that reunion brings, whether an adoption has been disrupted or not.

Plan for Emotional Times

Reunion, just like search, brings forth a number of unanticipated emotions in each of us. Some days, you will question yourself, wondering why you ever searched, regardless of the success or failure you experience in reunion. At times your emotions may shut down the progress of your search or communication with your birth family during the post-reunion process. The smallest piece of information can affect you in ways that will require you to withdraw for a while. If you know to expect these emotional shutdowns in advance, you can prepare yourself with a plan of action that either allows you to continue what you've begun from a distance, or provides you a break from the stress to recuperate before proceeding.

If you want to maintain either your search or your reunion (depending on which phase you are in), your plan might include designating a support person to carry on with some of the more rote aspects of the process.

Some of the more rudimentary tasks another person can help you with include typing and mailing letters you have handwritten, making telephone inquiries on your behalf, surfing the Internet adoption Web sites, and verbally supporting your need for a short break from birth family members whom you've already notified about this need. Be sure to empower your support person as your temporary spokesperson during your break, and while you are in emotional withdrawal, don't beat yourself up about being there.

The reality of reunion is that it always intrudes on the lives of both the searcher and the searchee. Unfortunately, the person searching becomes so intent on finding the person they are looking for that they tend to overlook the ramifications of actually meeting that person. Even positive reunions bring forth emotions that neither person can prepare for.

Unexpected Emotions

It took Jerry over seven years to find his birth mother, Grace. In retrospect, Jerry feels that he could have found Grace in about a year if he had been able to stay focused. He attributes the lengthy search time to the unexpected emotions unearthed by each new piece of information. For instance, when he received his medical records from the hospital where he was born, which listed his time of birth and the length of his birth mother's labor, he was elated. "I really was born and not hatched," he laughed. But the news also brought him sadness as he realized his birth mother had labored nearly twenty hours before he was born. "All that pain and suffering, for me! There was an irony to all of it, and it sent me into a long period of reflection and sadness. It's really just too difficult to even articulate all of the emotions."

Even with just his nonidentifying information, Jerry discovered strong connections to his biological family that did not exist within his adoptive family. He frequently stopped searching for six or eight months at a time just to absorb the information and deal with his emotions.

"Some days I was really gung-ho to get the search finished, and I would be on the phone to searchers, making contacts on the Internet, or writing letters. Other days I wasn't sure if I should be doing it at all. Sometimes I felt guilty about the possibility of intruding on Grace's life, or I worried about my mom and dad—how were they going to feel? Was I being disloyal to them and all they had given me in my life? So, I would just stop," he explained.

Overcoming the Stigma of Your Secret

For Grace, reunion was awkward at first. While she wanted to know what had happened to her son, she had never told anyone about her birth mother status. She was afraid of being rejected by her family because she had kept the secret for so long. Finally, her desire to include Jerry in her life helped her overcome her fears. To her amazement, her husband was very understanding, sympathetic, and supportive, acknowledging society's views at the time. Her children, Jerry's half-siblings, were also supportive and understanding. Her youngest son simply commented, "Cool. So, when do we meet our brother?"

Author and adoption reform advocate Carol Schaefer discusses similar emotions in her book *The Other Mother* (1991), which tells the story of the search and reunion with her son. Schaefer also experienced an emotional roller-coaster ride during both search and reunion. She became obsessed with locating her son and often experienced feelings of depression over the obstacles she had to overcome.

Beyond the obvious setbacks of search, Schaefer had two other children at home whose lives she had to keep balanced despite her own emotional setbacks. Support was often difficult for her to rally, and she frequently felt isolated and alone in her quest for knowledge about her son. Schaefer consulted not only a professional therapist, but also a psychic. Both were critical to her emotional well-being.

Schaefer's search was neither quick nor simple, but it was laced with amazing synchronicity, which she was only able to realize after meeting her son. For example, both of them ended up living in the same state, but she had surrendered him to adoption on the opposite side of the country. The resulting meeting also led to a friendship between Schaefer and her son's adoptive mother, whom Schaefer acknowledges as the "real mother" of her son's life (Schaefer being the "other mother"). Today she enjoys sharing grandmother status with her son's adoptive mother. Despite the difficulty of search and reunion, she believes all the expressed and denied emotions were a price worth paying for the release from fears reunion has brought her.

Reunion Realities

Susan searched several years for her daughter and was overwhelmed with joy the day she learned her daughter's identity. Her daughter, Jennifer, also seemed overjoyed at finally knowing about her birth mother. The two had frequent contact over the next few years, but every visit left each of them with a void that neither was able to verbalize to the other. They both felt simultaneously elated over being reunited and yet empty and conflicted. Susan was finally able to identify the emotion as "facing the realities of reunion."

Each visit with Jennifer made Susan painfully aware that the loss she experienced from relinquishment was never going to be entirely satisfied, despite reunion. She realized that she had been desperately seeking the baby she had lost to adoption, and reunion brought her a grown woman who could never fill the emptiness left by the loss of her infant.

Additionally, Jennifer was coming to terms with her own emotions. She had never had a close, loving relationship with her adoptive mother and had fantasized about finally securing that with her birth mother. But as reality set in, she wasn't sure if she could accept Susan as her mother in a traditional mother-daughter relationship. She had been independent of a family relationship for so many years that it felt awkward and uncomfortable to her, despite having fantasized about her birth mother being a part of her life.

Susan and her daughter independently sought the help of professional therapists to deal with their emotions surrounding their reunion. Although there can never be complete resolution for either Susan or Jennifer, the two are finally able to understand their emotions better. They have established a different type of love than either expected—a genuine friendship, a bond between two adults who happen to have a biological connection. It has been very satisfying for them.

They had walked on eggshells with each other since their reunion began, hiding their feelings of insecurity out of fear that the other one would be frightened away from the relationship. Susan and Jennifer accepted the risk in establishing a relationship, realizing that there were no guarantees for success simply because they were biologically related. They were willing to work hard to build the relationship to a level that was comfortable for both of them.

"Some things in life are just worth the extra work," Jennifer and Susan agreed. "And this was one of those things."

Since Susan had initiated the search, she had been reluctant to express her feelings of continued emptiness to Jennifer. "I had no idea that I would still not feel completion in my life after I found her," Susan explained. "I thought I would feel so fulfilled, but that didn't happen. The reunion actually made me feel worse because it brought back so many old emotions and also made me face what I had missed all those years and was never going to have."

The driving force that caused Susan to seek professional help to maintain the reunion was based on this lack of fulfillment. "While I was beating myself up emotionally for all that I had missed, I also knew that I didn't want to continue missing my daughter from my life."

Jennifer expressed similar feelings. "This whole reunion thing just wasn't what I thought it was going to be, you know, like what you see on television and stuff where everyone is so chummy and lovey," she explained. "But the older I get, the more I realize that few things in life ever are exactly how you dream they're going to be."

Because she'd been estranged from her adoptive mother for years, Jennifer had a strong desire to finally have "a mommy" in her life. But, until she was confronted with the possibility of having her true birth mother fill that role, Jennifer had never considered the complexities a real family life might bring.

"All of a sudden, there were all these people ready to be my family," Jennifer noted. "It was kind of overwhelming. I mean, one part of me was so ready for all they had to offer, but the other side of me was thinking, 'Hey—where were you when I really needed you, like, the day I was born?' Like I'm just supposed to ignore the fact that if these people had been supportive of my mom when she was pregnant with me and facing giving me away to strangers, we wouldn't be here having a reunion today because we would never have been apart."

While some of those feelings remain with Jennifer, she has been able to move forward with the extended family relationships because she has come to terms emotionally, with the understanding that they were all victims of the times.

"It was the 1960s," she said. "Unwed mothers just didn't keep their babies back then. It was a big taboo with entire families being made outcast by society if their daughter chose to be a single mother. Thank God, things are changing these days. Nobody should ever have to go through that kind of torture."

Susan and Jennifer have involved themselves in a great deal of soul searching throughout their reunion process. The heated emotions they each initially felt have subsided as time has passed, and they now feel very comfortable with each other and the relationship they have. Despite unfulfilled expectations, they both believe the knowledge they gained about one another has been very rewarding. They have determined that it's not *what* you find in reunion, but simply *that* you find.

Questions to Contemplate: How Will This Reunion Affect Everyone?

The birth parents and the adoptee aren't the only ones affected by reunion. Be sure to take into account *all* the people who matter to you. Ask yourself the following:

For Birth Parents:

- Am I prepared to invite the adoptee to be a part of my life, regardless of the circumstances the adoptee may be in?

- What circumstances could possibly prevent this from being a reality? What are my limitations of acceptance, if any?

- Is my family emotionally prepared for a reunion and how will it impact their lives?

- What happens if I disapprove of the adoptive parents? How will I handle this situation in order to ensure sensitivity toward the adoptee's feelings?

- How important is it to me that my child fulfills my expectationsl and fantasies?

For Adoptees:

- Am I prepared to meet a birth family who wants a relationship? Am I emotionally prepared if they are disinterested in me?

- What am I doing to educate my spouse and children about adoption issues?

- How do I envision the role of the birth family in my life? As family? Extended family? Someone I know? A friend? Not really anyone to be included in a meaningful way?

- What obligations do I foresee once I open the door of reunion? Am I open to meeting siblings? Grandparents? Aunts and uncles?

- Am I able to accept possible "total acceptance" and not feel bitter that I'm being received as a "long-lost child"? Or do I anticipate being treated as a visiting outsider, and prefer this?

- Am I anticipating the reunion to hold consequences for my adoptive parents and siblings? If so, what possible consequences could there be?

Chapter 4

Creating a Support System for Your Emotional Needs

It's important to recognize that emotional highs and lows are a normal part of the search and reunion process. Whether you have joined an adoption-related support group or simply have a good circle of family and friends, having a stable support system in place will make the emotional ups and downs more tolerable. People in search and reunion who seek help, either from a professional therapist or an adoption support group, agree that they are better able to cope with their adoption issues than before they secured help.

"I was floundering with my emotions and my search before I joined an adoption support group," Jerry said. "It was the first time I had met people who could understand exactly what I was feeling even though I wasn't always able to express myself. There's just something comforting about being in a room with a group of people and not having to say a single word to know that they genuinely understand what I am feeling."

Jerry and many other adoptees and birth parents have recognized the underlying need to be accepted by empathetic people during the search and reunion process. However, people who aren't searching may be apathetic or may even discourage you from searching.

"My husband was very supportive throughout my search and continues to be so in my reunion," Susan explained. "But other family members were not as accepting. In fact, some were adamantly against me finding my daughter. And as supportive as my husband was, he often was unable to understand what I was feeling."

Susan sought both professional and peer support. "The therapist helped me sort through the emotions I was experiencing and get into better touch with myself and reality. My support group was there to help me pick up the pieces, and they understood what I was experiencing without me ever having to express anything. They helped make things bearable."

Whether a person is in search or reunion, emotions can become overwhelming. For this reason, educating those closest to you is an essential factor. If they are unable to empathize or be supportive of your need to establish a relationship with your biological connections, your relationship with them stands in jeopardy.

How Do I Begin?

Regardless of your reunion outcome, support can be beautiful. It is important to surround yourself with people who will offer you as much compassion and patience as you are willing to give to the person you are seeking. If your immediate family is unable to meet your emotional needs for support, then it is advisable that you either join an adoption support group or invite other adoptees or birth parents to join your personal circle of support.

If you don't know any adoption triad members, issue a press release to your local newspaper's community desk, stating that you are seeking other adoptees and birth parents to form a support group. You will be surprised at the number of telephone calls you receive, as well as the type of people who respond. Adoption surpasses all boundaries of race, religion, and socioeconomic levels. It's amazing how people from varying backgrounds and cultures can share such intimate details of their lives without condemnation or judgment. Support groups are filled with compassionate, sensitive people who know exactly how you feel even when you are unable to articulate your thoughts.

Don't let your own lack of experience intimidate you—you can form an adoption support group of your own. Some simple guidelines follow:

- See details below about how to write your press release. Mail it to area newspapers and/or television and radio stations.

- Contact a local library, hotel, or restaurant and ask if they will donate a room once or twice monthly for your meeting.

- Write down the name, address, and phone number of each adoption triad person who calls you so you can contact them after a meeting time has been established, with your assurance that communications will be made discreetly and confidentially.

- Poll adoption triad members who contact you to determine the favored monthly meeting time, for example, first Saturday of each month or second Tuesday evening of each month.

- Mail out a press release to area newspapers and/or television and radio stations to announce your organizational meeting and all subsequent meetings two weeks prior to the meeting date(s).

- At the organizational meeting, ask for participants' input to determine a meeting format, for example, informal with/ without refreshments, organized with guest speakers, monthly topics of discussion, educational, collection of dues or no dues, etc. If you have not yet decided on a name for your group, you might consider suggestions at this meeting.

- Keep a logbook of attendees' names and addresses.

- Maintain the monthly or semi-monthly routine and enlist the aide of other support group members so no one person is overburdened.

A press release calling for the organization of a support group might look like this:

For Immediate Release: (date)

Media Contact: (your name and telephone number)

ADOPTION SUPPORT GROUP TO ORGANIZE

(Your City/State)—Adult adoptees and birth parents in the area are invited to participate in an adoption search and reunion support group that is currently being organized. A meeting date, place, and time will be determined by the response of interested participants. To become involved or for more information, call 555-555-0000 by (date).

-30-

(These specific numbers, with hyphens before the 3 and after the 0, indicate "The End." An alternative to indicate your press release has ended is three number symbols: ###).

After the response deadline has passed and you have some people interested in participating, establish a meeting place, date, and time, then mail out another press release notifying the adoption community at large. This second announcement might read as follows:

For Immediate Release: (date)

Media Contact: (your name and telephone number)

ADOPTION SUPPORT GROUP TO MEET

(Your City/State)—An adoption support group for Orange County has recently been formed and will conduct its organizational meeting in the conference room of Coleman Public Library on Saturday, May 25, from 9:00 to 11:00 A.M. Meetings are expected to take place on the last Saturday of each month, same time and location.

The group has been formed in an effort to provide adult adoptees and birth parents an opportunity to express their emotions about their own adoption and/or reunion experience in a confidential, compassionate setting without fear of judgment. Additional forms of education will take place at future meetings, enlightening participants to a variety of adoption issues and reform needs.

To confirm attendance or for more information, call 555-555-0000.

-30-

Future press releases should be mailed at least two weeks prior to the meeting date to announce the date, time, location, and topic for the month. Sending postcard reminders to past attendees is also a good idea if your group has the finances to support the mailings. Always be sure to request that attendees make either a cash or stamp contribution each month to cover mailing costs. Once your group is established, you can save postage by designating someone to call previous attendees to remind them of the meeting a few days in advance.

You might also consider contacting the American Adoption Congress (AAC) for support materials and handouts, as well as the International Soundex Reunion Registry (ISRR) for free reunion registry forms and information about national adoption support groups. Contact details for these and other organizations are listed in the Resources section of this book.

Support groups really do not require a lot of time on the part of the founding member. Once established, duties can be delegated so that no one person is overburdened. The benefits of participating in an adoption support group far outweigh the work required to form and maintain the organization.

The Internet's Role in Support

Until recent years, adoptees and birth parents experiencing search and reunion worked through their issues either alone, with a professional therapist, or in small support groups. The popularization of the Internet has changed the face of adoption support forever.

Dozens of Web sites provide the person in search or reunion numerous opportunities to converse, share ideas, rally emotional support, and gain valuable insight into adoption issues previously unheard in public. Online sites offer assistance in searches, as well as advice on methods of contact and reunion maintenance. The Internet can be a valuable resource for people in search or reunion to work through their personal issues and learn from other people's experiences—especially for the person who has no local support group and is left to meander the adoption course alone. These Web sites, news groups, and list servers can offer a lifeline or safety zone for expressing what otherwise might remain bottled up and internalized for decades, resulting in physiological problems.

Freedom to express yourself during this most emotional time of your life is vital. You must be able to express your frustrations, anger, love, and other emotions within a safe environment. While the Internet isn't the perfect medium for this, its convenience and anonymity are attractive to many.

The Internet allows participants the opportunity to vent their feelings while remaining anonymous (if they choose). The danger here is that the Internet, as wonderful as it can be, is not complete reality. While providing you with contacts, resources, and some feeling of security, it also has the potential to do exactly the opposite if caution is not exercised.

Once inside, you might find yourself criticized for your opinions, flamed for your input, and in a position of defense or disappointment. In opening up to a room full of strangers with no identities, you also leave yourself open for attack, and may find yourself on the offensive or withdrawing completely to regroup and lick your wounds.

In recent years, list servers, news groups, and Web sites have acknowledged the problems with "flaming" and request or warn participants to refrain from attacking other participants postings, reminding posters that everyone has a right to his own opinion. Unfortunately, as much as the server might try to prevent hurt feelings or rage from occurring, personalities are going to occasionally conflict and someone is going to go away mad. Know this in advance, and be forewarned when you enter cyberspace searching for support with your adoption-related issues. If you find yourself being attacked online for your ideas, try not to take it personally. Realize that the antagonist may be operating out of ignorance to your situation, or he may simply have his own personality difficulties, which you have no control over. Try to ignore the attack and move on, realizing that there are at least a dozen other folks online to support you versus the one stopping to antagonize.

Because of the anonymity and feelings of security, a lot of good advice and information is exchanged online. Frankly, our position is that the Internet is a valuable resource but shouldn't become your life. Use it to your advantage and, as in the workplace, don't take the issues home with you. For a list of some of the most popular servers, news groups, and chat rooms, see the Resources section of this book.

Questions to Contemplate: The Possibility of Rejection

Rejection may be constantly on your mind as you move toward reunion, or you may not have even let yourself imagine the possibility. Either way, it's important to do a little thinking on the subject—just don't obsess about it. Ask yourself:

- Am I emotionally prepared with a backup support system, in case I find that the other person is not interested in meeting me? Or does not engage as dramatically in the adoption reunion as I hoped?

- Am I prepared to find that perhaps the person I seek to have the reunion with is deceased, in prison, or otherwise unreachable for reunion?

- Have I checked into adoption support groups in my area that can lend support and understanding while I prepare for my reunion?

- Have I read as much as I can about the complexities of adoption issues, so that I have more insight into how the other person might feel?

- What would be my course of action for rejection? To continue to keep contact—hoping that the door would open? Drop all contact altogether? Sit and wait until contact is made, if ever?

- Have I examined all the possible emotional states that I might end up experiencing, examining each one of them in relationship to myself as a person? How do I deal with anger? Joy? Frustration? Disappointment? Happiness? Fear? Have I learned through the years what steps I can take to deal with unpleasant emotions? And, if so, what are they? Make a list.

- Am I prepared to go on with my life, understanding that it is not my fault if I'm rejected—people have to know me to reject me. It is the circumstances that are being rejected, not myself as a person.

- Do I recognize that projection of anger and fear are normal human defense mechanisms, but knowing their proper function is important to remain in control of yourself?

- Am I prepared to settle for perhaps basic answers to questions only, but not a relationship?

Chapter *5*

The *Stages* of Reunion

Like marriage, the reunion experience develops over time in stages, and no two experiences are identical. Reunion relationships are unpredictable and can't be controlled. There's no set time frame for you to measure while traveling the reunion trail. Some stages will seem to last a long time, and others will pass quickly.

While some professionals may disagree on the number of stages in reunion, and some adoption triad members won't experience all the stages, we have identified ten common phases that may help you to understand the process you're going through.

It's important to realize that these stages can happen in any order. And don't let the phase called "search" fool you. It might not seem applicable to you if, for example, the identity and location of the person you're seeking for reunion is known, as in cases of kinship or stepparent adoptions. But these cases still involve a search phase—it's just more likely to be within yourself, as you resolve your issues and emotions before making contact.

Although a specific order of approach isn't necessarily relevant, we have listed the stages according to what we feel is the most logical progression.

1. **Search**

    Every accomplishment in life begins with a first step, and this is what search is to most people seeking reunion. Search begins with a conscious thought or decision to gain more information about someone. This stage can be simple and quick or complicated and lengthy. If you begin your reunion with search, sometimes the last place you want to look is the place you should start: your adoptive parents. You may feel that your interest in finding your birth mother and father will be interpreted as being ungrateful or disloyal to the parents who raised you. So, instead of informing your parents about your decision to search for your biological family, you keep it a secret to avoid hurt feelings or conflict. Regardless of your triad position as either a birth parent or an adoptee, we advocate "no more secrets." Confide in your family. Tell them about your decision and ask for their support. They might just hold the key that will unlock your life story. Either before or after consulting your parents, contact every reunion registry available to you and put your name on their lists.

2. **Emotional Conflict**

   Once you have made the decision to search, you might begin second-guessing your decision, especially as you run into obstacles, like the lack of information available to you, or the discovery of lies and other false information. Your emotions will range from angry, sad, frustrated, and depressed, to happy, satisfied, and even joyously overwhelmed. Each new piece of information you discover will unleash an emotion. Be ready for this to happen. Expect your emotions to cause you to withdraw on occasion—from family, friends and even your search. Also, take care of your health by planning how you'll deal with the stress these emotions will bring into your life.

3. **Identities Revealed**

   There is the real possibility that you might never find the person you're seeking. You might never even know their name. But for many of you, an identity will ultimately be revealed. This, too, will cause emotions to swell. Remember that even the most joyous of occasions can bring on stress, so be prepared to take care of your health first.

4. **Initial Contact**

   What do you plan to do with the identity of the person once you discover it? Is it your goal to meet them? If so, how do you plan to initiate contact? By telephone? Letter? A knock on their door? Will you use an intermediary to make contact on your behalf or will you make direct contact yourself? Remember that first impressions are lasting impressions. Also, try not to speculate about the other person or how you will be received. You don't know one another. It has been a lifetime since you've seen each other, so you are literally strangers even though you are related by blood. Proceed with caution and respect for the other person's privacy.

5. **Acceptance or Rejection**—Once initial contact has been made, you will quickly know whether your overture is

welcome or if it's perceived as a threat. Everyone who seeks reunion desires acceptance. However, in reality, it doesn't always happen. Some people simply aren't ready for a reunion. Others are prepared to provide you with information but not a relationship. Sometimes their rejection of your efforts is permanent and sometimes it isn't. If you are met with rejection, we advise you to maintain objectivity and poise. Don't overreact in anger or with threats. Remember that you have opened the door to something unknown, and the other person might need time to adjust to the idea. Many people who were initially rejected were later welcomed into the other person's life. Once you dare to open the door to a relationship, leave it open if you have hope that someday the other person will walk through it.

6. **The First Meeting**
   If you get this far, consider yourself blessed. If you were going to be rejected by the person you found, chances are it would have happened before you set an appointment for your first meeting. However, remain cautious. A first meeting doesn't guarantee a lifelong relationship. Accept it for what it is—a meeting. Don't let the other person's willingness to meet you personally lead you to become cocky or presumptuous. Your attitude alone can be a potential turnoff and cause the person to withdraw from you. Keep in mind that you will be nervous at this meeting. Don't be afraid to let them know that in advance; it is almost certain that they share in your anxiety. When preparing for the first meeting, don't go into overkill mode. Be as relaxed as possible. A new haircut, new clothes, and new makeup are not necessary and may only add to your anxiety, making you less relaxed. Have confidence, and don't be pressured into changing anything about yourself for this meeting. Also, don't give into the temptation to bring a gift. It's too early in the relationship and might make them feel awkward or overwhelmed. If you're compelled to take something, take personal photographs from various stages of your life.

7. **The Honeymoon Phase**
   Everything will feel new during this stage of reunion. You may contact each other frequently and make trips back and forth to visit each other as you attempt to settle into your separate levels of comfort with the relationship. Once both parties are confident that the other one isn't going to run away, the intensity of the relationship calms down significantly. During this period of heightened emotion, it's easy to

be blindsided by your emotions and behave out of your normal boundaries. One of you might start acting overly giddy, nervous, talkative, or even presumptuous, which can make the other person feel embarrassed, nervous, silent, or otherwise on display. This is completely normal. Remember that you are both walking on proverbial eggshells during this stage, so be sure to cut each other some slack. Neither of you is deliberately trying to embarrass, make nervous, withdraw from, or display the other one—it just feels that way because of the newness and circumstances of the relationship. Also, you must realize that this stage of reunion isn't limited to just you and your reunion partner. If you have decided to establish a relationship, then this is the phase where you will be introduced to a lot of new people, testing the new relationship possibly to its limits. But being part of family life typically involves other people besides the two of you.

8. **Post-honeymoon**
As the relationship moves out of its honeymoon phase, you may be overwrought with emotions. You may even feel that it's your fault that the other person has reduced the frequency of contact. In the post-honeymoon phase, participants often try to second-guess what the other person is thinking and feeling. Likewise, you need to appreciate what you've been able to accomplish in the relationship. And, like a typical family, sometimes there is frequent contact, and other times there is distance and pause. As you realize that frequency in contact has nothing to do with the love you feel and/or receive, you will move through this stage of emotional conflict and finally feel comfortable in your relationship.

9. **Resolution**
When your emotional conflict has subsided and you feel calm in your developing relationship, you will also finally be able to resolve issues with yourself, as well as about the other person. Resolution doesn't necessarily equal forgiveness. The scars of relinquishment for each individual are such that forgiveness can't be presumed. There are some birth mothers who don't seek forgiveness because they fear that in doing so, they would be absolved of their own responsibility in relinquishment, and they aren't comfortable doing that. There are adoptees who are willing to establish a relationship with their birth mother and/or father, but their hurt or anger is so deep that total forgiveness might never come. So, don't enter a reunion expecting forgiveness—it's

not easily obtainable. Instead, be open to what resolution can bring you: acceptance.

10. **Post-reunion**

When all is said and done, sit back and say a prayer of thanks to everyone and everything that contributed to your reunion and the relationship you have developed with one another. Maintain mutual respect, open communication, and integrity, and you will discover that your reunion has become just another aspect of your life. You will feel a measure of success when friends ask "How's your daughter?" or "How's your birth mother?" and you actually have an answer for them. Remember, though, that reunion relationships are subject to the same pangs and problems as any other friendship or family relationship. Reunion bonds are possibly a little more fragile than others because of the circumstances under which they were forged. Always be prepared to give the other person any distance they might need throughout your relationship; don't presume anything, and always consult them before making plans that include them. If they hesitate or renege on a plan, don't automatically assume that "something's wrong." After all, people do change their minds occasionally, and things genuinely come up. Extend the benefit of the doubt to the person you're in reunion with, just as you would another friend.

United Through Adoption: A Different Kind of Reunion

Julie Bailey shares a unique reunion story:

Either physically or cognitively, reunion is inevitable for every adoptee and birth mother. Whether or not you generate a search, the first fantasy you have or question you ask about that unknown person unites you emotionally. The stages of reunion are set into motion at this point, even if the search phase remains locked in your dreams and the remaining stages play out in the privacy of your Ghost Kingdom. For some questing triad members, this is as far as they will ever go in reunion. Others will walk the razor's edge of reunion for possibly a lifetime, pretending to be content, denying their desire to know more, balancing between initiating a physical search and not wanting to be perceived as disloyal. This is where the person becomes stuck in the emotional conflict within the stages of reunion. If you find yourself in this position, it is advisable to work through your issues and move on.

Having a confidant with whom you can discuss ideas and issues helps your emotional balance. Sometimes it takes the views and observations of an outsider to help you identify or articulate your own perspective and objectivity throughout the stages of reunion, from thought to action. My friend Gail was that for me, just as I was for her.

When I met Gail in 1980, we both knew instantly that we were going to be the best of friends. We were drawn to each other like magnets. As our friendship developed, we found so much common ground that Gail used to joke, "We could plant quite a garden on this soil!"

Although my work was in public relations and hers was in graphic design, we complemented each other tremendously, each of us sharing a natural tendency toward the other's profession. Many times over the years we would work late to help the other one meet a deadline. Sometimes we played hooky from work and went off to go horseback riding, picnicking, fishing, or shopping at flea markets. I believe the similarity that bonded us the most was the fact that she was an adoptee and I was a birth mother.

Even though Gail was my age, I was able to view the adoptee's world through her eyes; I looked at her and imagined that my own relinquished daughter was as happy in her life. My relationship with Gail gave me hope for my own child. Gail had a wonderful life and was raised by two very loving, nurturing parents. I was privileged to have known them both and to have been included in numerous family activities.

While Gail didn't have the same deep need to know her birth mother that I had to know my daughter, she told me often that she was comforted by just "knowing a birth mother never forgets and always holds the child she relinquished in her heart." She was very supportive of my need to find my daughter and shared many tears with me over the years. She remained adamant, though, that she didn't have a desire to search for her birth mother. She couldn't imagine more love in the world beyond what she had received from her parents, and she also didn't want to invade her birth mom's privacy or create any discomfort or sadness for her by making contact. Gail remained content, happy, and emotionally healthy about her own unique completeness and rarely expressed curiosity about her biological heritage.

Ironically, it was her own adoptive mother who encouraged her to find her "real family," as she called them, and it was Gail who corrected her with, "You are my real family." Hearing Gail speak those words brought me to the saddest and yet most loving of realities. The "real" parents and family of children—adopted or otherwise—are the people who raised them. This reality, while temporarily hurtful to me as a birth mom, was the truth. I came to terms with it quickly.

I know the insights we gave to one another were invaluable to us both. Gail stopped referring to her relinquishment as having been "given up for adoption" because of my intense dislike for the phrase. I used to tell her it made it sound like it was all my idea, or that I voluntarily made the choice, willingly and happily. I might give up my seat on a bus or in a crowded auditorium to an elderly person or give up my serving of dessert—gladly, as a gesture of help and courtesy. But I did not give up my daughter as any gesture of courtesy or to be helpful. She was "relinquished" or "surrendered" with a great deal of remorse and emotional suffering involved.

Although some people don't see the differences, they are crucial to me. "Relinquished" and "surrendered" connote some sense of sadness, emotion, or other act of desperation. It's important to exercise sensitivity with adoption terminology. Using words out of context or inappropriately can cause the other person to withdraw from the conversation. So, try to keep not only an open mind, but also an open ear to maintain respectful communication. The ability for Gail and me to do this created a lifelong, loving relationship for us both, and good friends are key ingredients to measuring a successful life.

I still remember the day Gail called me in tears to tell me that her mother, while under anesthesia for a surgical procedure, had told Gail her birth mother's name. She confided to me that she couldn't believe the emotions evoked by just hearing a name. Never in her life had she thought she wanted or needed to know anything about her birth family until she heard the name spoken aloud. Now, filled with emotion, curiosity, and a burning desire to know more, Gail decided to search.

Unfortunately, Gail's mother became seriously ill, so Gail's attention had to be focused on her mom rather than her search and potential reunion. Her father had died a few years earlier, so she was intent on spending every available moment with her mother, even moving her in to live with Gail and her family.

The year or two of illness passed quickly. Several months after Gail's mother passed away, Gail started having intense visions. She saw her mother walk through the room, had conversations with her—genuine déjà vu. My husband and I had moved 600 miles away, but Gail and I kept in touch regularly. Finally, her visions became so overwhelming that Gail went to see her doctor.

The diagnosis was quick and devastating. Gail had brain cancer. The surgery was successful to an extent, but they weren't able to remove all the cancerous cells. Because of this, doctors inserted a radioactive disc in her brain, hoping it would kill the remaining cancer cells.

Gail's visions didn't completely stop, but at least the neurologist was able to give her an understandable explanation: The tumor was attached to the area of the brain where memories are stored and he believed this was the root of her déjà vu.

The threat of a terminal illness returned Gail's interest to a reunion with her birth mother. She asked me to help her search, and I did. In retrospect, I don't know if Gail had me initiate the search because it was important to her, or because she knew it had been important to her mother and to me as well. She was that kind of friend. If she knew something was important to you, she would often lay aside her own ideas to make your desires a reality.

I went to see Gail in June of 1998. She was semi-conscious and slow to respond. I still didn't have the identity of her birth mother and felt as though I had completely failed my dear friend. I left her and went back to the phones in a last-ditch effort.

When I returned to Gail's house the next morning, she was in a coma. Her hospice volunteer and nurse were there, talking about Gail's strong will and ability to hold on to life despite everything else giving out. The volunteer said, "I'll bet she's holding on for a word from that friend of hers who's helping her locate her birth mother." It took me a minute to realize she was talking about me. I consulted Gail's husband and placed one last call.

Bingo. A name and a phone number. Her husband asked me to make the call. "This was something between you two," he said. "I think you need to be the one to finish it." And I did.

If you think introducing yourself to your birth mother is a difficult, awkward task, try making the call as an intermediary to tell the birth mother that her daughter is literally on her deathbed. There are no adequate words to describe how nervous I felt. I was so afraid of failure, but thankfully, it didn't come.

Gail's birth mother, although devastated about Gail's condition, was grateful to know what had happened to the baby girl she had been coerced into relinquishing forty-five years earlier. She had never told her subsequent children about having surrendered a daughter for adoption, and wasn't sure what she should do at this juncture.

I told her that I hadn't made the phone call to force her into making a decision. I made the call because my best friend had asked me to find her birth mother and tell her, "Thank you for having had the courage to let me be adopted." Gail wanted her birth mom to finally be comforted about her past and know that Gail's life had been filled with blessings and love.

When I hung up the phone, I returned to Gail's bedside and told her about the phone call. Gail had been lying in bed all day, comatose, unable to move and unresponsive to all outside stimulus, expressionless, motionless. Regardless, I had to tell her about having spoken to her birth mother.

"Gail," I started. "I just hung up the phone with your birth mother. Her name is Lila. I told her everything you have always said you wanted her to know. I said that you were raised by two of the best people God created, that your life was filled with love and happiness, and I thanked her for you, for her having had the courage to place you with your parents. She wanted you to know that she never forgot you, Gail. She hopes you can forgive her for not being able to raise you, and she hopes you understand that she truly felt you would have a better life with someone else. I told her that you did, Gail, and that seemed to make her happy."

As I spoke these words, the facial expression on my comatose friend changed. It wasn't a muscular reaction. It was the same face I see on every adoptee and birth mother just after they've learned the name of their biological family. Through her disembodied state, somehow, Gail heard and acknowledged. She was crying with joy over the news.

Gail passed away the very next morning around 7:00 A.M. I miss her very much.

When Life Separates

You came into my life like a breeze—
Always cool, always unpredictable, always refreshing.
You didn't merely extend your hand in friendship
But, rather, embraced me as a soulmate;
Two familiar spirits who will remain as such forever.
We shared our secrets and bared our inner selves;
You, always making me welcome in your life,
Me, always moving somewhere or another—
But remaining bonded to each other, regardless.
We two, who know the deepest meaning of reunion
Shall one day find ourselves in reunion—together.
I miss you.

—Julie Jarrell Bailey (1998)

Questions to Contemplate:
The Many Facets of Adoption

General Questions:

- What are your basic views on adoption? How will these views affect your reunion?

- Are you prepared to honor the other's convictions regarding the adoption process, without feeling pressured to compromise yours?

- Do you have angry feelings when you think of the adoptive parents? Or your birth parents? Have you worked through these feelings, if present, by attending workshops and support groups, and by involving yourself with others who have walked this path?

- What is the middle meeting ground you think might result from a reunion? Your opinions will evolve and change over time, so this is a good question to revisit often.

For Birth Parents:

- Do you hold "adoption" responsible for the loss of your child? And will these feelings, if present, be negatively perceived by the adoptee and/or their family?

- Are you secretly hoping the adoptee holds the same views on adoption as you, perhaps even hoping to find you are needed because the adoption failed? Or would knowing that your child had a happy home bring you happiness?

- Would you be disappointed if your child referred to you by your first name rather than Mom? Are you hoping she will consider you her "mother"? Or are you prepared to be a friend, if that is the role that follows?

- Do you believe you were "misled" into believing you couldn't parent your child? Do you believe the reunion represents the opportunity to "reclaim"? Or are you willing to allow for a new form of family to evolve, which can redefine itself after a reunion?

- Would you be insulted or angered if you found the adoptee were an activist for open records, although you had been a silent person who resented intrusion? Would you be able to accept the adoptee's passion with understanding, or would this be outside your comfort zone?

For Adoptees:

- Do you believe that the birth family can have "family ties" with you? Or is adoption black and white—all or nothing, with everything having already been said and done?

- Would you be angered if you learned that your birth parent was vocal in speaking out against current adoption laws, despite you having had a happy experience?

- Do you believe that adoption is a good societal institution, and were you "glad" you were adopted? Does this belief, if you have it, allow room for "extended birth family" members?

- Do labels bother you? Would you be offended if your birth mother meets you and immediately calls you "her child"? Would you perceive that as an affront to your adoptive parents, even if your birth mother didn't mean it that way?

Part **2**

Practical Advice for Sidestepping Reunion Pitfalls

There is a newness and a rebirth
In giving to others what you most need yourself.
There is magic in a prayer, a thought, or a focus
For another person
And through such thoughts
The world will change—not in a day
But in a moment
In a breath.

—Tom L.

Chapter 6

Overcoming Barriers

When you begin the search for your biological connection, you may have one or several reasons for seeking a reunion. these are just a few of the reasons adoptees and birth parents search for one another:

- To satisfy a curiosity about the other person

- Out of an overwhelming desire to *know* (not simple curiosity)

- To make a connection with something greater than oneself—one's biological heritage

- For medical reasons including the need to diagnose difficult symptoms, terminal or life-threatening illness, mental illness, or information exchange for future generations' needs

Do any of these sound familiar? Regardless of why you wish to find the person you're looking for, the fact remains that you will have to jump some emotion hurdles as you go through the process. There are few statistics on adoption search and reunion, and those that are available are often controversial due to the low number of participants. In research intended to determine the numbers of adoptees and birth parents desiring a reunion with the other, as few as fourteen participants have been included in a sampling, which does not adequately represent the adoptee or birth parent community. Questionable statistics indicate that more than 25 percent of the adopted population is interested in knowing about their biological heritage, but that number is believed to be low because of inadequate sampling of triad members. Some members of the AAC speculate a higher sampling would raise the figures significantly.

Regardless, these low samplings and statistics haven't deterred the person intent on finding from searching. Statistical analysis isn't something adoptees and birth parents engage in before looking for one another. They aren't concerned about the other searches and reunions out there. They are only interested in one—theirs.

Moving Beyond Emotions

You may be wondering just how a person can get past all of the stigmas and emotional obstacles reunion might bring. While each case must be determined by its own unique set of circumstances, there are some relatively simple guidelines that can help most people in reunion.

Utilizing some common sense and imagining your self in the other person's situation is always the best and easiest advice. We asked the experts—adoptees, birth parents, and adoptive parents who are currently living in reunions—to provide suggestions to help you overcome some of the emotional barriers you might face. Here are the topics they came up with and related suggestions:

Free Yourself from Fear

Don't let your fear of the unknown or the past consume you and prevent you from making contact. The worst-case scenario is that you might be rejected, or you will find that the other person has died. If either of these happen, draw on your inner strength and your support circle to survive the wound and move on with your life. Although it's unpleasant and emotionally difficult, rejection is survivable and can actually be a great learning experience. As one adoptee rejected at reunion said, "Reunion is a crap shoot. I might have lost at this hand but tomorrow I'll win at something else. That's life."

Knowledge Is Power

Do your homework before rushing into reunion. Learn a few things about the person you're making contact with, either via a private investigator, an Internet search, or a neighbor (discreetly, without identifying your motives). Neighbors and coworkers are often eager to share information. In other words, try to learn a little about what is behind the door that will either be opened or shut in your face. This information will give you insight about the other person and help you make a plan for the best approach method, or help you decide a better time for contact. Something to watch out for here: If you disclose to them just how much you learned about them prior to contact, they may feel vulnerable or threatened. Use discretion and keep what you learn to yourself.

Don't Make Demands

When you finally do make contact, be careful to not make demands of the person you found. Insisting that they provide you with information, introduce you to family, go public with your reunion, etc., can only turn the relationship sour.

Regardless of your position in the adoption triad, you should always respect the privacy and need for confidentiality of the other people involved. Remember that they might never have told anyone about you, so it might be extremely embarrassing for them if you contact other family members, like siblings or spouses. It might also result in your relationship being terminated—and that is not the goal of reunion.

Limit Your Expectations

Adoptees and birth parents live in a fantasy world for decades. Don't let your fantasies define your expectations. Otherwise, you might find yourself emotionally devastated.

Banish Guilt Trips

Women who relinquish children to adoption—if they are in reasonably good mental health—always live with some form of guilt, remorse, or general feelings of inadequacy. Refrain from trying to get your financial or other personal needs met by feeding off this emotional state. Whatever gifts might be exchanged throughout the years of reunion will come naturally after a level of comfort has been achieved.

Empower the Person You Find

Give them control by allowing them to choose the pace and direction of the relationship. People who have been shocked or surprised often feel that someone or something else is in control of their lives. They become defensive, which can cause them to withdraw while they try to regain composure. Talk to the person. Assure him that although you were the one who initiated contact, you are turning the reins over to him and giving him control over the direction of the relationship. At that point, you need to back off and give him the opportunity to reconnect with you. As tempting as it will be, remain silent until you hear from him again.

Some adoption advisors disagree about continuing contact when your attempts have been ignored, but we believe each case has unique situations and personalities involved. You should evaluate your own situation and determine the appropriateness of attempting contact one more time. If you decide to try again, use logic and discretion. Don't badger the person with letters and telephone calls until their only response can be, "Leave me alone!" We advise waiting at least a year before writing them again, and only a quick postcard or note, preferably in recognition of a special holiday or birthday. Simply state, "Thinking of you and hoping you are well. In case you lost my address and telephone number, here's how you can reach me. . . ." Nothing more. If they haven't been in contact with you, then the last thing they'll want to hear is an outpouring of your love for them or any attempt to make them feel guilty for their silence.

Be Honest

Answer questions honestly. Nobody likes to feel they were deceived. The following are some subjects about which adoptees and birth parents sometimes feel a need to tell only half-truths:

- *Paternity*. If you, as the birth mother, had intimate relationships with more than one man and you're unsure of the birth father's identity, admit it. Better yet, volunteer the information before you are asked. Times have changed and indiscretions are not judged as harshly today as in the past.

- *Disclosure of mental illness and emotional/behavioral disorders*. Seeking psychiatric help today isn't the social taboo it was twenty-five years ago. A great deal of research shows these disorders have a genetic component, so they should be disclosed as early as possible in the relationship. The same goes for any physical health problems.

- *Prison term or other legal problems*. This is a subject most people prefer to keep secret, but be assured it will be discovered at some point in time. Prompt disclosure will prevent the other party from feeling deceived or caught off guard when someone else mentions it. Also, don't let anyone use information about your past, regardless of its specifics, to emotionally blackmail you. Confession can be good for the soul and within its freedom a great relationship might grow.

- *Substance abuse*. Past substance abuse (such as alcoholism or drug addiction) may seem irrelevant at first, but with so much research to support a genetic propensity for addiction, this information can be very important to the adoptee, regardless of whether or not the birth parent is currently involved in substance abuse. Likewise, for the adoptee with substance abuse difficulties, admitting the truth to your birth parent may offer you some supportive and surprising answers to put you on the road to recovery.

- *Your feelings*. Reunion affects everyone around you. Don't let hurt feelings and conflicted emotions grow quietly within you. Remember that reunion is completely new ground for all parties involved; sometimes you are not going to like what the other person is doing and vice versa. Instead of living silently with the conflict, it is better to express your thoughts so they can be resolved quickly.

- All of you involved are truly reunion pioneers operating in undiscovered territory. The more verbally expressive each one of you is, the quicker everyone will achieve his or her own level of comfort in the relationship. Adoptive parents typically suppress their emotions in reunion because they want their child to be happy. In addition, adoptive parents tend to be the people whose feelings get hurt the most as they watch their child dancing off in the moonlight with strangers—even worse, strangers who have the biological connection to the child that the adoptive parents don't have. Friends also tend to distance themselves during reunion simply because they don't know what to think or say. Reunion is virgin territory to the people outside the triad, so if you're hoping for input from them, you will probably have to ask or invite them to share their feelings with you.

Chapter **7**

Essentials for a Successful Reunion

Perhaps the biggest myth surrounding adoption reunions is that suddenly your life will be complete. While it is true that another person can add new dimensions to your current life, it is not true that your life will be complete once you meet the person you're searching for. Often, it has quite the opposite effect.

Adoption reunions are not a state of mind, but rather a declaration from the heart, and this is where dreams are most often shattered. Reunion is a flawed state simply by virtue of what came before it: Lies were told, secrets were maintained, records were sealed, and lives were devastated, all in the name of adoption. These relationships can be very fragile and should be handled with extreme care—not just as though you're walking on eggshells, but on cracked eggshells, which you must be careful not to shatter completely.

Guidelines for reunion relationships involve little more than basic common sense. It's true that you can't prepare yourself emotionally for everything reunion might bring you. There are too many unknowns in adoption, and regardless of the safeguards you put in place, you still run the risk of being hurt. But the more safeguards you have initiated, the more likely you are to survive the crisis.

Reunion Aerobics: Essential Exercises

One of the surest ways to survive and succeed with your reunion is by exercising what we call *reunion aerobics*. Reunion aerobics require that you exercise caution, compassion, responsibility, and patience throughout your reunion.

As your reunion progresses, you will discover information that offers you at least two or more options for proceeding. It is a bit more complicated than the obvious, "right" or "wrong" methods. Reunion involves so much undiscovered territory that you will often feel overwhelmed. Some of the obvious variables to consider include age, health, economics, social standing, and education. The not-so-obvious variables will include things like family dynamics, personality, religion, mental illness, greed, personal desires, and so on.

It is important that you come to terms with your emotional limitations before making contact with the other person. If you have no idea how you might react in a worst-case scenario, then you are setting yourself up for failure and devastation. For example, what would you do if you found your birth mother or your daughter, only to discover during the initial phase of the relationship that she had a mental illness or brain damage, and had only a limited ability to function in society?

Watch Out for Pitfalls

Iris's adoption fantasy was based on the information her caseworker had provided her after her daughter was born. The caseworker told Iris that her daughter was being adopted into a wonderful, well-respected family of substance, who would provide her daughter with everything that Iris was unable to guarantee. She said everything Iris needed to hear in order to feel comfortable about relinquishing.

Over the years Iris dreamed of her little girl playing in a big yard with a handsome swing-set and lots of toys. She envisioned her little girl dressed in fancy clothes and having perfectly groomed hair with a big pink bow. The fantasies changed according to whatever age her daughter was at the time, concluding with a college diploma, a professional career, and a happy family life.

Iris never had other children. She began the search for her daughter hoping to fill a void within herself. She dreamed about their reunion and how wonderful it was going to be.

When Iris finally located her daughter, she neglected to exercise her reunion aerobics during the contact process. She did not proceed with caution, compassion, responsibility, or patience. Tragically, none of Iris's fantasies about her daughter were ever a reality. She learned that her daughter, Sissy, had been brain damaged during birth and delivery. Although she functioned normally on a physical level, the brain damage had left her with varying degrees of behavioral and mental disorders that made her a difficult and often impossible personality.

Sissy had been institutionalized for many years due to her uncontrollable behavior. When the two met, Iris was shocked to see a young woman who looked twenty years older than her actual age. Sissy appeared disheveled and behaved in a wild, threatening manner, which concerned Iris. Sissy told Iris unbelievable tales about her life, which only served to make Iris feel guilty and depressed. She left the meeting wishing it had never taken place and cursing herself for not having prepared herself for a negative scenario. A few days following the initial meeting, Iris contacted Sissy's adoptive brother and learned the entire story of mental illness due to the brain damage, as well as Sissy's entanglements with the law because of her psychotic behavior.

In retrospect, Iris realizes she would have handled the reunion differently if she had been able to contain herself and utilize the reunion aerobics. Like so many other people in search, Iris allowed her emotions to lead her rather than her common sense, resulting in an overwhelming situation. Her workout toward reunion could have included:

- Taking time to digest the information and either making a better plan for contact with Sissy, or deciding to be satisfied with the new knowledge about her daughter (rather than to risk upsetting both of them).

- Enlisting the services of the local mental health agency to provide help and assistance for Sissy that Iris was not able to handle emotionally or literally.

Due to the overwhelming feelings of confusion and conflict, Iris could only move ahead with a second meeting. This time, Sissy's behavior was even more erratic. She came with a list of demands for Iris, which were surprising and financially unfeasible. Then she threatened to hurt Iris physically if she wasn't given everything on her list. In the end, Iris asked Sissy to stop calling, telling her that she was unable to be the "mommy" that Sissy expected. It was a very emotional moment for Iris because she had very much wanted to be a mother to her lost daughter. Tragically, Sissy became verbally abusive and so threatening that Iris eventually changed her telephone number, finding comfort that she had never given Sissy her home address.

We've used the devastating example of Iris and Sissy's reunion to demonstrate an extreme. Reunions of this type are rare because they can be avoided by exercising caution, compassion, responsibility, and patience. Most people approaching reunion go to extremes to learn everything they can about the other person prior to making contact. Some searchers fear rejection or that the initial contact may be all they get, so they engage in a little extra detective work in the event that the information they secure prior to contact is all they ever get. Some other people in search reach for more information simply to satisfy a natural curiosity, or end up with it because they hired a professional, whose fee included more detailed information. In any case, the more information you have, the better prepared you will be to make contact. In spite of all you may learn about the other person, it is advisable to allow them to tell you things about themselves without you interrupting: "Oh, yeah. I heard that about you from the private investigator I hired to find you." Comments like this will only serve to make the person you found feel like their privacy has been completely invaded, with a resulting defensiveness that may damage the reunion process. It's advisable for you to keep some details of your search process to yourself.

As mentioned, Iris and Sissy's reunion was a negative extreme. Most reunions proceed through normal stages: contact, introduction (either face-to-face or less personal medium), eggshells phase (emotional), honeymoon phase, resolving issues or conflicts and settling into reunion on your own comfortable level (regardless of the other person's comfort).

Warning Signs

It is important to remember that some reunions, regardless of the positive aspects of reflection or fantasy, just do not work out. Despite this knowledge, adoption researchers conclude that 1.8 out of every 4 adoptees want to search for their biological families (AAC Decree, 1998).

So, how do you determine if your reunion is going sour? What essential indicators will provide you the clues that it's time to simply move on? Beyond the obvious, there are other signs that a reunion isn't working out to your ideal. Some signs are subtle, while other indicators glare at you like a neon sign.

The most obvious indicator lies with your letters, telephone calls, or visits being rejected; even worse would be if you received an injunction to "cease and desist" your attempts to make contact. If you see your reunion explode on television as the person you found is interviewed on behalf of upholding closed adoption records, that's a sure sign your reunion has problems. Something similar happened in May 1999 when the ABC television network show *20/20* aired a segment entitled "Mothers in the Shadows," with interviews conducted by Connie Chung.

The show featured birth mothers who had initially been receptive to having been found, but when personalities conflicted on one level or another, they chose to terminate the relationship. They came out of their shadows to protest state referendums will open sealed birth records. The following are two of the stories they told:

- One birth mother complained that her daughter was insensitive about the rape that resulted in the daughter's birth. The adoptee wrote and asked the birth mother for information about her birth father, which caused the birth mother to terminate the exchange of letters and photographs. Apparently, there was unresolved fear on the part of the birth mother that through their daughter, her rapist would be able to harm her again.

- Another birth mother initially seemed happy to hear from her daughter. She later severed contact, offering no reason the adoptee could relate to. The adoptee described her birth mother's action as "cold." Regardless, the adoptee respected her birth mother's decision and ceased all contact with her. Four years later, the birth mother sued the private investigator who had located her, citing that her "privacy was invaded." The shocked adoptee decided to attempt a face-to-face meeting with her birth mother and showed up on her doorstep with a German television crew, but she still did not get the meeting or answers she had hoped for.

Guidelines to Follow

As we dissect these attempted and severed reunions, it is easy to determine when and where things went wrong. Hindsight and a television show transcript make the process easy. In review, some suggestions support group peer counselors offered include:

- Be patient when entering a reunion. An initial letter or telephone call that seems to have been happily received is no assurance that the reunion will last forever.

- Do not force your attentions on the other person. If your first letter or telephone call is not reciprocated, do not proceed further. Even if your first few letters or telephone calls seem to be received favorably, do not move too fast by initiating contact between communications. Always wait to hear from the other person before proceeding with additional contact, as tempting as it might be for you to press forward. The exception to this would be sending a card—no gift—for special occasions, such as birthdays and holidays. Skip the flowery messages—just a simple "thinking of you" will get your message across.

- Behave responsibly by utilizing some commonsense guidelines. If the person you are contacting has been the victim of a violent crime, be sensitive. Validate their emotions. Empathize. Offer to suspend communication for a while, allowing the other person more time to digest all that he or she must be feeling. Try to put yourself in the other person's place and proceed in the manner in which you would prefer to be approached.

- Do not contact the media to record your reunion. The media might very well accommodate your request, especially during sweeps periods. Your reunion will be exploited for ratings with little regard to the potential damage publicity will do. Always remember that newspapers and television stations edit reality to fit an allotted time. The story you might dream of having publicized will never be accurately told, unless you buy your own advertising space and edit everything yourself. Regardless, it is wiser to keep reunions—which are matters of the heart, not ratings—private. Leave the reporters out of it.

- Remember that every time a reunion horror story is featured in the media, it instills emotional terror in someone, which may prevent them from ever being able to open their heart and life to a reunion. People react in different ways in an effort to feel secure, and that is something that can never be predicted. This is not only another good reason to keep your reunion out of the media; it may also help you understand skittishness on the part of other triad members.

Even with all the media coverage of reunions gone bad, most triad members who decide to search are willing to accept the risk of rejection and other emotional setbacks (Giddens 1998).

Finding the Right Approach

Cindy was in her late forties when she decided to search for her birth mother. Through the nonidentifying information she received from her state's Office of Vital Statistics, Cindy was able to piece together a trail of information, which led directly to her birth mother. Unsure of what to do next, Cindy turned to an adoption support group for advice. The support group helped by forcing her to look within herself and determine what it was she was truly seeking. Cindy had always thought she would be completely satisfied with just knowing the name of her birth mother, but now that she had the name, she wasn't sure if this simple knowledge was satisfying enough to her. What should she do?

Cindy decided that contact with her birth mother, Geneva, might be too overwhelming for them both. She felt it was important to exercise caution, as well as conduct herself responsibly if she decided to make contact. As Cindy listened to other people's reunion stories and became aware of the complexities involved, she chose to make contact through an intermediary.

Although Cindy expected rejection, she chose to proceed with contact because she wanted to relieve any pain Geneva might have suffered in wondering about her all those years. She instructed the intermediary to tell her birth mother, "Thank you for having the courage to choose adoption," apologize for the intrusion, and explain that Cindy's intent was simply to give Geneva some peace of mind in the event that she needed any solace over the relinquishment. She instructed the intermediary to provide Geneva with Cindy's name, address, and telephone number, and to invite her to call Cindy if she ever wanted contact or a personal meeting, emphasizing that the next move would have to come from Geneva.

Nearly three months later, after Cindy had finally settled into the idea of having been rejected by her birth mother for the second time in her life, Geneva telephoned. She apologized for taking so long to call, explaining that she had just needed some time to digest the news. Geneva wasn't sure how to proceed or even if she should proceed, she explained to Cindy, because she had never told anyone other than her husband about Cindy's birth. She didn't know how she would explain Cindy to her children or other family members, but she was grateful that Cindy had let her know she was well, and she hoped for some photographs of Cindy if possible.

Cindy quickly reassured Geneva that she was not about to divulge her secret, and gave her permission to proceed or not proceed with the relationship at her own pace.

"Phone calls like this can really raise a person's defenses," said Cindy. "I knew that if I had any chance at a relationship with my birth mother, it wasn't going to work if I ran to *Oprah* or the local media with my story."

Through reflection and self-evaluation, Cindy came to realize that all she had been seeking was an exchange of information and to set her birth mother's mind at ease in the event Geneva had ever felt remorse or guilt over surrendering Cindy for adoption. A relationship might have been nice, but Cindy considered that to be the proverbial "icing on the cake," not the goal of search.

In the end, Geneva provided Cindy with valuable medical history. The two exchanged photographs and have kept in contact annually at Christmas with cards and updated photos. Cindy doesn't know if she will ever meet Geneva face-to-face, but considers their reunion to be successful and is content with the way it has progressed thus far.

Cindy proceeded with caution and discovered she had compassion for this woman who had given birth to her. She no longer felt the pangs of abandonment, and this helped her to conduct herself responsibly throughout the reunion process. As she continues to exercise patience, she believes the reunion will evolve further. But even if it doesn't, she is content with the knowledge she has gained.

Regardless of the outcome, most lessons learned throughout the reunion process are by trial and error. While it is good to listen to the stories of those who have driven the reunion road before you, don't base your own expectations on their realities. Thoroughly examine any fantasies you might have about your own reunion. It is easier to make adjustments before making contact than to have to scramble afterwards.

Chapter **8**

Tools for the Journey

I believe that anyone can conquer fear by doing the things he fears to do.

—Eleanor Roosevelt

Fear is a natural element of the reunion process. There are many contributing factors for fear, but in adoption, it is primarily based on fear of the unknown. Will I be rejected? Will they like me? Are we going to lose our child once they meet their birth family? Everyone involved needs reassurance that life and love will last through the reunion.

Confront Your Fear

Reunion should be embraced, not feared. Through reunion, many past fears and curiosities can be put to rest for all three members of the adoption triad. The information we gain from reunions provides us the opportunity to make decisions for ourselves and to move on with our lives. Knowledge of self is not something you can learn about in a book. It can only be learned by facing your fears and by ongoing self-examination.

Fear of the Unknown

Reunion can bring out the best or the worst in everyone concerned. It unlocks emotions that have been buried for decades. Once the decision to make contact is made and the process begins, you will probably find yourself imagining some aspect of the effort with an uncommon negativity, fearing the worst.

Realize that experiencing fear or anxiety about making contact is normal. Fear of the unknown—primarily, fear of rejection—can actually prevent you from making contact even when you have the other person's name, address, and telephone number. You might find yourself trying to second-guess the reactions of the person you seek, and you'll probably discover a few of your own issues of self-esteem as well. These are just a few of the questions we have heard adoptees and birth mothers worry themselves over:

- Will she hate me for surrendering her?

- Will he think I'm too fat or ugly to want a relationship with me?

- What if he's dead?

- Will I be rejected because I'm gay (or lesbian)?

- What if she is mentally handicapped or has some other disability?

- What if she can't accept my disability?

- What if he's in prison, an ex-convict, a drug addict, or an alcoholic?

- What if he is a sex offender?

- What if I'm not good enough?

If you aren't feeling a little paranoid and questioning yourself at this point, count your blessings. Most people who reach this point in the journey toward reunion experience feelings of inadequacy, insecurity, and general fear. A few do not.

Involve Your Family

It is essential that you make every attempt to get your family involved in your reunion process, starting with your search. Keep them informed as you progress. Help them to understand the various emotions you feel, such as depression, elation, impulsiveness, anxiety, and guilt. Assure everyone that your desire and need for a reunion are not about them, but rather about yourself and your need to have some lifelong questions answered.

Remember that your family and friends aren't mind readers. You are responsible for maintaining an open line of communication with the people you care about most. Help them recognize their importance in your life, regardless of whoever else might enter the picture. Be sure to thank them when they are supportive and be assured that they are the ones who will stick by you in the long run, even if your reunion does not progress as you had hoped.

The reunion process, like search, can be very threatening to people outside the triad who are close to you. Suddenly, your lives have a new element added—and it's not something simple like changing jobs and meeting new people. Reunion has a deeper sense of transition and far-reaching dynamics. It rises from the essence of your soul, not a job résumé, and it will require a great deal of work.

Evaluate Your Prejudices

Any of the above listed fears could be true. However, the more constructive question to ask yourself is, "How will I react, and what are the limits of my acceptance?" The advice here is to examine yourself thoroughly before you make contact. Come to terms with your own limitations, prejudices, and abilities before invading the life of this stranger who is so intimately attached to you.

It is advisable that you formulate possible reunion scenarios and make a plan of action for each. For example, imagine that when you find your birth mother you discover that your birth father had raped and brutalized her and you are the product of that crime. Make yourself a list of multiple choice options for reactions you might experience, such as:

a. I will expect her to embrace me and welcome me into her family.

b. I will want her to give me as much detail about my birth father as she can remember so I am able to find him in the future.

c. I will let her know that I am alive and well, and will offer her the opportunity to receive photographs and other communications without being intrusive.

d. I will offer her my sympathy and ride off into the sunset embarrassed and confused about having made any contact with her.

Be sure to include happy reunion scenarios in your options, because not only do they exist, they happen more often than rejection (Giddens 1998). The objective is to make every attempt to prepare yourself for every potential outcome. Also, remember to remain flexible in all of your reunion responses, because as prepared as you think you are, something will surely arise that you hadn't considered.

Decide What You Can Give

Imagine that you initiate a search because you want to offer some peace of mind to your birth mother in the event she had ever experienced remorse or depression over having relinquished you, and because you would also enjoy having a more complete medical history. However, you aren't looking to establish any long-term relationship with her. When you finally locate your birth mother, her openness and desire to make you an active participant in her family overwhelm you. This is not what you had anticipated at all. You . . .

    a. Sit her down and tell her you cannot be involved on this level because it is not something you are emotionally equipped to do.

    b. Ignore her telephone calls and letters, hoping that she will just go away if you ignore her long enough.

    c. Accept her unconditional love with surprise and joy, and work hard at maintaining a lasting relationship.

    d. Allow her this honeymoon phase of reunion, knowing that in time the intensity will die down and you will all adjust to something on a more comfortable level.

    None of the above options are incorrect. If it is right for you, then you simply determine the best method to exercise your reunion aerobics: caution, compassion, responsibility, and patience. The first two reactions listed above might be hurtful, but if you proceed with compassion and behave responsibly, either can be achieved with limited disappointment.

Be Patient

If you are the person who has made contact, then you must allow the other person time to absorb the situation. Their initial reaction may be the opposite of what you had anticipated. Expect it to be that way.

After all, you have had a great deal of time to adjust to the idea of a reunion. You have just dropped a bomb in their laps and they have had no time to prepare themselves. Be sensitive to their needs and allow them the opportunity to feel in control of whatever is to happen next.

After contact is made, there is no turning back. Even in cases of severed reunions, there is no way to erase the knowledge of that other person. While disrupted reunions are a reality, they occur less frequently than long-term reunions. You can decrease the potential for a disrupted reunion by exercising your reunion aerobics.

Regardless of the reunion outcome, find comfort in knowing that you are not alone in the process. You have friends and family members to support you, as well as choices to make regarding the direction and continuation of contact.

Release Control

For some, this may be the first time in their life that they have felt completely in control of their destiny. Many adoptees report lifelong feelings of powerlessness because choices were always made for them, from the moment of birth when the birth mother chose relinquishment and the adoptive parents chose the child to build their family. Reunion gives adoptees and birth mothers the opportunity to choose or not choose contact. It returns control to the two people involved who felt powerless when the adoption originated. It provides adoptive parents the opportunity to help their child, and possibly bring closure regarding many questions that could never be answered prior to reunion.

Set Ground Rules

Each individual involved in the reunion process will need to decide on the level of contact that is most comfortable for him, and must be able to discuss it openly with the other person. If you are an independent person who prefers to keep a safe distance, then weekly telephone calls, letters, or visits are not for you. Should your reunion partner be a clingy person, the two of you will need to agree on guidelines.

Don't feel intimidated about setting ground rules for your reunion. If you are the person who initiated contact, remain flexible and tolerant of the other person's wishes—and try not to feel rejected if they want less frequent contact than you do.

Trust Your Instincts

Any relationship between two people can only last if both parties are willing to participate. If either person begins to feel awkward, intimidated, or simply overwhelmed, a relationship will be hard to build and sustain.

In other words, if the fit is comfortable, like a pair of good shoes, it will wear and last for a long time. If you try to build your relationship based on how you have seen other adoption reunions grow, your relationship will probably fail. It is folly to believe that your reunion relationship will be as wonderful or as awful as someone else's.

Trust yourself and your own instincts, because you know yourself better than anyone does. It is great to listen to friends and family who want to make suggestions or comments about how to proceed with your reunion. But don't ever let someone talk you into proceeding with your reunion in any manner you find awkward or uncomfortable. That doesn't mean you should ignore their advice; sometimes they can offer you objective words of wisdom. Ultimately, however, you are the one who must live with your actions.

Prepare for the Worst—Pray for the Best

A difficult aspect of writing this book has been in the area of sharing the negative potential reunion holds. Our goal is not to scare you, but to present both sides of reunion so you can better prepare yourself and experience the greatest joy and the least pain.

While not everyone has a perfect reunion, and some are rejected, you will have the most potential for success because you are working to prepare yourself for imperfections. As you immerse yourself in reunion stories and discover why some work out better than others, you will be able to make plans to either overcome or cope with your own potential reunion outcome.

Some reunions might never be fulfilled due to lack of preparation, an abrasive or intrusive approach with the other person, or, just as likely (and completely uncontrollable), emotional instability on the part of the other person. A reunion relationship can't be sustained without work, even if all you're seeking is infrequent contact. While not every reunion will be happy and lifelong, all reunions are successful in the new knowledge gained by both parties. The longevity of a reunion relationship is not a measure of success.

Respect Rejection

Realize that one sure way to doom a reunion is to relentlessly pursue someone who wants to remain anonymous. To show up on their doorstep uninvited and unexpected is the worst plan you can make in this situation. However, show that same person respect and compassion—even back off, distancing yourself while inviting them to re-establish contact in the future as you exercise patience waiting for them—and you have a better chance of hearing from them again, despite their initial desire for anonymity.

Be warned, though, that the person you seek might never be prepared for a relationship with you. If you convince yourself before you make contact that this is what will happen, you will cushion yourself from potential disappointment.

For some people, the wound of relinquishment is so deep that they will never be ready for reunion. Still, it may be that in your case the person has been waiting for you to make contact for years and you will be welcomed with open arms. Either way, you must have no expectations for a relationship and you should refrain from making demands of the person you find.

The Face of Rejection

Brenda was thrilled to have been so happily received by her birth mother, Georgia. The relationship was progressing better than she had ever imagined, despite Georgia's insistence about not revealing her long-kept secret to her family members. But one day Georgia telephoned Brenda and told her never to call or write to her again, because she had decided she couldn't maintain a relationship. The news devastated Brenda. She pleaded with Georgia to tell her why the relationship was ending. Had Brenda done or said something wrong? But Georgia wouldn't tell Brenda anything other than she didn't want to continue in the reunion, and she warned her not to make contact again unless she was prepared to deal with Georgia's lawyer.

Brenda had no idea what happened, so she could only speculate. It took her a very long time to come to terms with the loss of their reunion and feelings of having been abandoned a second time by the same person. After a few years, however, Brenda realized that she had nothing to do with the failure of the reunion. It was Georgia's choice, for whatever reason, and as Brenda now relates her story, she adds, "It's her loss, because I'm a pretty nice person to know."

Regardless of the reunion's outcome, Brenda is glad she found her birth mother. "I had a lot of questions answered for myself, and I wouldn't trade what I've learned for anything in the world."

Brenda's attitude regarding the failure of her reunion is admirable—and it's the advisable path for you to take as well. She realized that sometimes there can be no understanding—no way to discover why something happened as it did. At times such as this, it is best to move on with your life and not let the sadness consume you.

Your self-worth is as important as that of the person you sought. Don't beat yourself up over their lack of sensitivity or inability to sustain the relationship. Always conduct yourself with a high level of integrity so that if the time ever comes when one of you must become the proverbial "bad guy," that it's the other person and not you to assume the role.

Chapter **9**

First Contact: How Do I Do That?

So, you finally completed the hard part of your search. You thought it was terribly difficult because it was filled with so many emotions, riddled with questions, encumbered with obstacles, and over-whelmed with frustrations. Well, brace yourself: That was the easy part. Now that you have a name and address for the person you searched for, the truly hard part is about to happen.

You are going to make contact with them.

What Are My Contact Options?

There are only a few methods to choose from when it comes to mak-ing contact. You can reach them by telephone, in writing, in person, or via an intermediary. So, how do you decide which method of con-tact is the right one for you? That's a bit tougher. If you poll every-one you know who has had a reunion, you will probably find that the answers are pretty evenly distributed.

Deciding on your method of contact is something only you can do. The key is to evaluate your level of comfort. Are you better at expressing yourself in writing, or do you prefer the spontaneity of the telephone? Do you prefer to lay all of your cards on the table in person so your unknown family member has to accept or reject you face-to-face? Are you shy or overly emotional? If so, an intermediary is a good choice.

The worst decision that you can make is to let someone else make the choice for you. They aren't you, regardless of how well they might know you, and ultimately, you're the one responsible for this first impression and the one who will be most affected by it.

If you aren't comfortable talking on the telephone, then don't let someone convince you to place a call. Likewise, if you find that writing provides you the opportunity for the clearest thought and lets you present yourself in the best light, then go for it. Regardless of your choice, remember these tips:

- If you get an answering machine, DO NOT leave a message. Call back until you get a human being.

- When you get the person you want on the telephone, be courteous. Introduce yourself, tell them you have a private matter to discuss with them, and ask if it's a good time to call. If your timing isn't good, ask for a day and time that might be better.

- Have a friend or family member with you when you telephone in the event that you become too emotional to talk.

- If you write a letter, be sure to mail it "certified" or "registered" so a signature will be required from the person to whom the envelope was addressed.

- Don't frighten the other person away by sounding too possessive or needy in your first contact. Refrain from being overly sentimental and using phrases such as, "I've loved you since the day you were born," or "I've wanted you in my life forever," or other intimate family terms.

- If showing up on the person's doorstep is your choice—one we don't recommend, although it's the most comfortable option for some folks—then make sure you are talking directly to the person you've been searching for before beginning your speech.

- Choose an experienced intermediary whose personality is similar to yours—someone you can genuinely trust to represent your best interests with integrity and intelligence.

- Stay involved. If possible, be with the intermediary when she makes the phone call. If you have someone else write a letter for you, edit it to your own style before mailing it.

- Don't dump a bunch of new personalities on your reunion partner immediately. Give them time to get to know you before you introduce them to their extended family.

Because you have your own unique style, first contact needs to be initiated with your own personality and comfort level in mind.

And remember, everyone feels nervous at this point. It's completely natural; thousands have traveled this road before you and have experienced the same anxiety you are feeling.

Regardless of the method of contact you choose, be thoroughly prepared. Here's some advice on getting ready:

Telephone Call

Write yourself a script of your ideal conversation. This way, you've played a scenario in your head and have a general idea of how you would like to see things flow. Divide a sheet of paper into two columns. On one side, list questions you hope will be answered. On the opposite side, list information you want to be sure to tell the person. Check them off as you proceed through them in the conversation.

How do you start the telephone conversation? Make it as generic and nonthreatening as possible. Here's a sample script for contacting your birth mother:

You:　　　　Hello, Mrs. Bailey? This is Marshall Goodson. You don't really know me, but I recently acquired some sensitive information and I wanted to talk to you about it. It's rather private in nature. Is this a good time for you to talk uninterrupted?

Mrs. Bailey:　Sure. What's this all about?

You:　　　　First, do you have a pencil and paper handy? I want you to write down my name and phone number in case we get cut off for some reason. [provide your name and telephone number] Mrs. Bailey—I'm calling in regard to an adoption that took place in 1968 that I have reason to believe you were involved with. I'm trying to verify some of the information I've received.

Mrs. Bailey:　Why would you think I would know anything?

You:　　　　I recently received some documents that included your name on them, Mrs. Bailey. I know this phone call is a surprise to you and I want to put you at ease. Nobody is in any way trying to upset you or intrude upon your privacy any further than this call, and I know just receiving this call might be upsetting to you. I apologize for that. I hope you understand that I've been wanting to meet my birth mother for a very long time—and all of the information I've received points to you as being the woman I'm searching for. Can you help me here, Mrs. Bailey?

At this point in the conversation, you will know if the person to whom you are speaking is going to accept or reject you. Her response will either be honest and open or she will deny what you've told her. There have been cases where the birth mother has hung up on the adoptee as soon as she realizes where the conversation is leading; it's rare, but it has happened. Most often, you can expect the person to listen to you and answer your questions. If the woman has been praying for this day for years, she will quickly confirm that she is the one you've been seeking.

Know this, however: Even if she denies knowledge of your birth it doesn't always mean that you've reached the wrong person. Remember that birth mothers have been conditioned to deny the child they relinquished, so in many cases, an unexpected phone call like this will put her instantly on the defensive. She may deny everything, and may or may not listen to you patiently and empathize with you. That's why it's important to have her write down your name and telephone number before you reveal the purpose of your call.

There have been reports of women who have lent their names to a friend to use in a maternity home or hospital situation, and just as many women who simply list false names that might be the same as the woman to whom you are speaking. Be prepared to give her the benefit of the doubt, regardless of your information. Errors and incorrect data have been at the base of many investigative conclusions.

Don't let her denial intimidate you from gathering more information from her. Ask her to brainstorm with you about the past, including trying to determine why her name might have been on the information you received. She might actually have a lead for you that can help, even if she isn't the right person.

Recognize when to back off, and do so politely. Always thank the person for talking to you, and ask them to keep your name and number in the event any ideas come to them.

Writing a Letter

If you decide it's more your style to write a letter rather than place a telephone call, we have some tips to guide you through that process, too. Adapting the letter to your own style is important, but there are a few essential elements to be sure to include.

First, we recommend that you include everything you had hoped you would be able to say to your birth mother or child within the contents of your letter. While some people might disagree with this, we recommend it because it might be your only chance to ever communicate with the person. We don't advocate teasing them in an attempt to get them to make contact. It might backfire on you, and then what do you have? Everything you really wanted them to know about you is lost because you thought you could entice them with bits of news, like dangling a carrot before a horse.

Don't sign the letter in an intimate way. This is your first contact and intimacy from you can be threatening to the other person. Remember to mail your letter "certified" or "registered" and "return receipt requested."

Also, include a self-addressed, stamped postcard, prewritten so that all the person has to do is check a response and mail it back to you if they don't want contact. A recurring complaint we hear from people in search is that the person they wrote to never responded, so they didn't know if they got the correct person or not. A few scribbled lines on a postcard that is already stamped can save you months of worry in the end. Enclosing a postcard is no guarantee they'll even mail that, but it does increase your chances of hearing from them one way or another. Write something that requires their response, such as:

Please return this postcard as soon as possible so I will know how to proceed. Your attention to this matter is greatly appreciated. Complete the following statement by checking the most accurate response:

❑ *I'm sorry, but I am not the person you are searching for. If I can think of anything that might be of help to you, I will contact you. Good luck.*

❑ *I am the person you are looking for. However, I am not prepared for a reunion at this time. Please respect my privacy and do not contact me again. I will keep your name and number in case I someday change my mind. (Optional: I will mail you medical information, as you requested, in the near future.)*

❑ *I am the person you are looking for, and I am open to a reunion at this time. Please call me at your convenience.*

In the event you have more than one prospect, be sure to code the postcard so you will know which person on your list mailed it to you.

As mentioned, the sample letter below is basic information and should be customized to your own style. It is meant to provide you with ideas on how to personalize your own letter. The first letter is written from a birth mother to an adoptee.

Dear Sally:

This letter might come as a shock to you, and for that, I apologize in advance. You see, I have recently received information that leads to you as my most promising suspect. I believe you are the daughter I relinquished for adoption in 1965. If so, you were born on May 1, 1965, at Memorial Hospital in Jacksonville, Florida. Your adoption was handled by Catholic Ministries of Duval County. You were four days old when I last held you in my arms.

When you were born, my life was in turmoil. I had no resources to keep you and adoption was the option I was assured would provide you with everything in life that I was unable to give you at the time. Although the years and towns have kept us separated, you have always remained close in my heart. I have waited to contact you until now because that was the promise I made to your adoptive parents and our caseworker when you were born.

An influencing factor in my contacting you now comes from seeing so many adoption reunion stories on television and in the media these past few years. It constantly brings my thoughts to you. I have heard many adoptees say they want and need updated medical information to help them, and I believe that is a reasonable request.

Let me assure you that I am not writing in an effort to interfere with your life or invade your privacy in any way. I am simply responding to the cries I have heard from other adoptees and want to be as supportive to you as possible. I have included a separate sheet for you, listing all currently known medical information for everyone in my family. I hope you will find this helpful.

Beyond the medical information, let me tell you a little about your other biological connections. I have included a few photographs for you to keep in the event you have any interest.

Birth father: (name and any current information you might have)

Siblings (half or full): (names, ages, current information)

Grandparents: (names, ages, living or deceased)

Me: (your full name, age, marital status and spouse's name, current information, e.g., type of employment, hobbies and interests, etc.)

(Other personal information or the story of her birth would be appropriate to follow here.)

Again, let me reassure you that I am not writing with any intention of invading your privacy or forcing you to meet me. Any meeting we might have will be by your own choosing. I want you to know that I am hopeful and open to meeting you in person, if you ever think you might be ready for it. If you're never ready to meet me face-to-face, I will be disappointed, but it will still be your choice. I will simply revel in the knowledge of your identity and hope that you are happy and healthy.

After taking time to digest the information within this letter and recover from the shock of hearing from me, I hope you will consider calling or writing to me, even if only once to tell me to leave you alone. Whatever your choice, I have enclosed a stamped and addressed postcard on which you can simply check the appropriate statement. I ask you to at least send me the postcard rather than ignore me so I don't drive myself crazy wondering if I'll ever hear from you. As you can imagine, this entire process has been very emotional for me, as I know it must be for you.

I look forward to hearing from you in one form or the other. I hope you enjoy the photographs I have enclosed. I wish you the best life has to offer.

Fondly, (or Sincerely, or Always, but not "Love")
(your name)

A letter from the adoptee to a birth mother might look something like this:

Dear June:
I am an adoptee and searching for my birth mother. I have recently received information that has led me to you as my primary suspect for being my birth mother. I was born May 1, 1965, at Memorial Hospital in Jacksonville, Florida. The agency that handled my adoption was Catholic Ministries of Duval County. If you are my birth mother, as I believe you must be, then this information is already familiar to you.

Let me assure you that I am not writing this letter in an attempt to invade your life or your privacy. I am writing to let you know that I have had a happy life, and that I have experienced minor health problems. I hope you are willing to provide me with an updated medical history, which will benefit not only me, but also your three grandchildren. If you are able to do this, I can only tell you that it will be a welcome relief to finally stop writing "unknown" on medical forms when I am asked to complete them.

I also want you to know that if you should decide you want to meet me that I am open and ready to meet you, too. But if that's not something you are ready for, I am able to respect your decision. I will certainly be disappointed, but, I realize that not all people are ready for personal meetings in reunion and some people need more time than others. Some people might never be ready—and that's okay, too.

Let me tell you a few things about me and my life. I have always known I was adopted. I also have two adopted brothers. Our parents were very loving and nurturing, as they continue to be today. I have had a good life, achieved moderate success and feel content. I have been married for 12 years to George, and we have three children; two boys, ages 6 and 10, one girl, age 4. George is an accountant at a hospital and I am a registered nurse. My parents, Alice and David, own their own business—a hardware store, in Atlanta. Like George, they have been very supportive of me finding you.

I have enclosed photographs for you and I hope you enjoy them. I have also included a postcard that you can mail back to me so I know your intentions regarding the pursuit of a relationship. Please mail the postcard as soon as possible so I don't drive myself crazy wondering if I will ever hear from you. The postcard has options for you to check off regarding your decision. Thanks for returning it to me.

I am sure all of this is a bit overwhelming at the moment. I apologize if I have upset you. That was not my intent. Please know that I have thought about you often over the years, as I'm sure you have thought about me. I hope I will hear from you, but if not, I promise to respect your privacy. You will not hear from me again until I hear from you.

I wish you the best and hope this letter has in some small way brought you comfort and a sense of peace.

Fondly, (or Sincerely, or Always, etc., but not "Love")
(your name here)

Once first contact is made, both of you will need to make a decision about meeting each other: when, where, how or even *if*. Some reunion participants are anxious to meet very soon after first contact, while others move into it slowly. We know one birth mother whose daughter took more than a year to respond to her initial letter. They were two years into their reunion before they ever met. So many variables are factored into a person's decision to meet face-to-face that it's impossible to guess what will happen. Reasons for hesitation expressed to us have included health problems, financial difficulties, a pregnancy, job-related commitments or stress, family illness, and other overwhelming emotions.

Once you both decide to meet one another, try not to let your anxiety and anticipation consume you. Approach the meeting as you have everything else in your relationship: with caution, compassion, responsibility, and patience. Choose a location where you will both be comfortable and relaxed. Discuss in advance the identities and number of people who will be accompanying you to the meeting. If you aren't comfortable having others at your first one-on-one meeting, don't be afraid to tell the other person your feelings. Some adoptees and birth parents feel the moment is too personal to share, while others are ready to include extended family and friends. Whatever your decision, keep communication open, express your needs about the meeting place, and do everything necessary to ensure comfort for you both.

We don't recommend making last-minute changes in yourself in an attempt to improve on Mother Nature. This is when things inevitably go wrong and result in you feeling self-conscious about meeting the other person. If you want to buy yourself a new outfit, that's okay, but buy something within your current personal tastes. Don't purchase something that simply isn't you, hoping to impress the person you're meeting. Just like a bad haircut, frizzed perm, or unflattering hair color, clothes that don't fit your normal level of comfort will prevent you from feeling relaxed during your encounter.

To Hug, or Not to Hug

Should you greet and/or leave your reunion companion with a hug? What level of affection is expected? These are questions commonly asked by adoptees and birth parents. Everyone is treading on eggshells and feeling self-conscious about everything.

Chances are that if you are a demonstrative, affectionate person, the person to whom you are genetically connected is also, and if you aren't typically touchy-feely, they probably aren't either. Regardless, hugs, kisses, and other expressions of affection are something you will have to play out on a gut level.

If giving the other person a hug feels right, then hug them. Remember, however, that there is a difference between offering a simple hug and being too clingy. Avoid overkill.

Here's another tip: If you're really undecided about how to handle being affectionate but don't want to appear aloof, then approach them with an extended arm for a warm handshake while patting their right shoulder with your left hand. That can be perceived as affectionate and respectful without being overwhelming to either person.

Part **3**

The Tangled Web of Rights and Legal Issues

The law must be consonant with life. It cannot and should not ignore broad historical currents of history. Mankind is possessed of no greater urge than to try to understand the age-old questions: Who am I? And, why am I? Even now, the sands and ashes of the continents are being sifted to find where we made our first steps as man. Religions of mankind often include ancestor worship in one way or another. For many, the future is blind without sight of the past. Those emotions and anxieties that generate our thirst to know the past are not superficial and whimsical. They are real and they are "good cause" under the law of man and God.

—The Honorable Wade Weatherford
Circuit Court Judge, South Carolina
(CERA Position Paper 1997)

Chapter 10

What Provisions Does My State Make for Reunions?

The quest for one's identity is not new to this generation or even this past millennium. Man has sought answers to questions concerning his own identity since the beginning of time. When his lineage is clearly identified, the connections and answers may be complex in philosophy, but they are simple to trace.

Only in modern times, and primarily only in America, are some children denied access to knowledge of their lineage and culture. Other great nations have either always had open records, or in recent times created methods of contact between family members who were separated by adoption. In the United States, however, reform has been slow in developing and has met with a great deal of controversy generated by people who support secrecy and silence in adoption (as we've described in earlier chapters of this book).

Controversy at the State Level

Oregon is just one of four states that recently opened its adoption records. The move prompted much media attention, so you're probably familiar with this case. The three other states that have opened records lately are Tennessee, Delaware, and Alabama. Each state was able to open their records either by legislative vote or referendum vote. Regardless of their method in achieving openness, each state has been subjected to a number of appeals or other suits by organizations and individuals or small groups who want to keep adoption records closed. Oregon was in the limelight because Justice Sandra Day O'Connor refused to block measure 58, which was passed by voters two years before it took effect. The new law provides adoptees age twenty-one years or older access to all of their birth records and at least the possibility of connecting with their birth parents.

A group of birth mothers in Oregon had sued to block the law under the premise that it violates the perceived promise of privacy they received when surrendering their children to adoption years earlier. They believed that opening records would also reopen old and painful wounds, as some of the women had been victims of rape.

At this writing, adoption records are legislated state by state. While six states now offer full access by individuals to their personal adoption records, many other states provide adoption reunion registries and/or intermediaries. Some systems require a court order before a participant may utilize the service, while others simply charge a fee.

There are two types of registries: passive and active. An example of a passive registry is the nonprofit International Soundex Reunion Registry (ISRR). A person registers, and when the person they are seeking also registers, they receive a telephone call or letter confirming the other person's identity.

Active registries work differently. With an active registry, only one of the parties (party A) involved needs to register, at which time a confidential search is initiated. When the person being sought (party B) is located, they are given the choice to either have or not have their identity disclosed to party A. If party B is found to be deceased, the information is usually released to party A, depending upon the guidelines mandated by their state.

An intermediary system works much like an active reunion registry, but the duties of the intermediaries are expanded—they act as a liaison for communication between the two until both parties are in agreement to meet. Confidentiality is maintained throughout all of these processes.

Although a growing number of states have defined reunion programs, a few remain completely closed, with no access to records and no reunion registry.

Reference Terminology and Abbreviations

The following terms will help you decipher the information in the state-by-state listings below:

Active registry: When you register with the specified agency, they conduct a search on your behalf, and they determine whether the party for whom you are searching desires contact, before they release any information.

By court order (BCO): The legal process to gain access to closed adoption records; usually based on "good cause," such as a medical emergency, documented medical need, or terminal illness. A need to know is rarely considered good cause and is left to the discretion of the court judge.

Contact preference: Similar to the contact veto, the contact preference is a document registered with the designated state or county agency by either of the parties, stating their preference to not be contacted. There are no legal ramifications in place to dissuade someone from violating a contact preference.

Contact veto: A document registered with the state/court refusing contact by either the birth parent or adoptee. A fine or other legal charge sometimes applies as a deterrent to discourage violation of the veto.

Disclosure veto: A document registered with the state/court disallowing the release of any personal or identifying information.

Intermediary (or Intermediary System): A third-party intervention process; either an individual or an agency/department approved by the courts to make contact with the person being sought on behalf of the person searching. The intermediary system is similar to an active reunion registry.

Nonidentifying information: Basic information about the person for whom you are searching, most often limited to age, race, hair/eye color, general profession or work status at time of relinquishment, and medical history known at time of relinquishment. There is no standard format for nonidentifying information, so states can mandate at their own discretion or determination of the law.

No provisions: A state system that provides no access to birth certificates or adoption records, and does not provide any form of registry or intermediary system for reunion contact. Even the release of nonidentifying information would be at the discretion of the individual or agency holding it.

Original birth certificate (OBC): An adoptee's nonamended birth certificate recorded at birth. It includes the identities of his birth parents.

Passive registry: A system in which both the adoptee and birth parent (or siblings) must register before identifying information can be released. Some states also require approving signatures from adoptive parents and/or both birth parents prior to releasing information.

Pending legislation: A bill that has been introduced and is awaiting final vote or other procedural analysis before becoming law.

Waiver (or Waiver of Confidentiality): A document filed by an adoptee or birth parent allowing the release of identifying information and records.

Below you will find a state-by-state listing of provisions to aid in adoption-based reunions. We have made every effort to include up-to-date information, but with laws constantly being challenged and new bills introduced, it is recommended that you contact your own State Department of Human Resources to inquire about the current status of adoption reunion options.

To use the listing below, look up the state where the birth relinquishment occurred. The first clause provides status on open records, followed by other pertinent information, including the department name, address, and telephone number to contact for additional information, such as queries about applicable registry fees or necessary forms. States whose open records are only accessible by court order will be listed as such, followed by whatever form of registry is provided, if any.

The Status of Adoption Records

Alabama: OBC. Open records passed May 2000, with HB690 allowing full access to records for adult adoptees. Appeals might be forthcoming. Contact: Department of Human Resources, Office of Adoption, S. Gordon Persons Building, 50 Ripley St., Montgomery, AL 36130. (205) 242-9500.

Alaska: OBC. Full access to records at age eighteen for adoptees; passive registry for birth parents. Contact: Department of Health and Social Services, Office of Adoption, Pouch H-05, Juneau, AK 99811. (907) 465-3191.

Arizona: BCO. Intermediary. Contact: Department of Economic Security, State Adoption Department, Administration for Children, Youth and Families, 3001 W. Indian School Rd., Phoenix, AZ 95017. (602) 277-3564.

Arkansas: BCO. Intermediary. Passive registry. Contact: Department of Human Services, Division of Social Services/Adoption Services,

P.O. Box 1437, Slot 808, Little Rock, AR 72203. (501) 682-8345. Note: A volunteer mutual consent registry is available. Call (501) 203-1437 for details.

California: BCO. Waiver system. Contact: Department of Social Services, State Adoption Department, 744 "P" Street, MS 19-31, Sacramento, CA 95814. (916) 973-3827.

Colorado: BCO at age eighteen. Birth parents contact veto. Passive registry. Intermediary. Contact: Department of Social Services, Post Adoption Services, 1575 Sherman St., Denver, CO 80203. (303) 866-5700.

Connecticut: BCO. Intermediary. Contact: Department of Children and Youth Services, Adoption Resource Exchange, Undercliff Rd., Bldg. 3, Meriden, CT 06450. (203) 238-6640.

Delaware: OBC at age twenty-one. Birth parent contact veto. Active registry. Contact: Department of Children, Youth and Family Services, Attn.: Adoption Coordinator, 1925 Faulkland Rd., Wilmington, DE 19805. (302) 633-2655.

District of Columbia: BCO (no provisions). Contact: Department of Human Services, Adoption and Placement Resources, 609 "H" Street, N.E., 5th Floor, Washington, DC 20002. (202) 727-5930.

Florida: BCO. Passive registry. Intermediary. Department of Health and Rehabilitative Services, Adoption Reunion Registry, 1317 Winewood Blvd., Bldg. 8, Room 100, Tallahassee, FL 32301. (904) 488-8000.

Georgia: BCO. Active registry. Contact: Department of Human Resources, State Adoption Unit, Room 501, 878 Peachtree St. N.E., Atlanta, GA 30309. (404) 894-2641.

Hawaii: OBC at age eighteen for persons adopted after 1991 with no disclosure veto on file. Pre-1991: Active registry. Intermediary given 120 days to obtain waiver from birth parents. If unobtainable, adoptee gains access to records without restrictions. Contact: Department of Human Services, Adoption Department, P.O. Box 339, Honolulu, HI 96809. (808) 548-2211.

Idaho: BCO (no provisions). Contact: State Department of Health and Welfare, Adoption Department, 450 W. State St., Boise, ID 93720. (208) 334-5697.

Illinois: BCO. Active registry via confidential intermediary. Original birth certificate can be obtained with mutual consent of adoptee and birth parents. Contact: Department of Children and Family Services, 406 E. Monroe, Springfield, IL 62706. (217) 785-2519.

Indiana: BCO, except adoptions prior to 1940, who have full access to records. Passive registry. Intermediary. Contact: Department of Public Welfare, Social Services Division, 141 Meridian St., Indianapolis, IN 46225. (317) 232-4956.

Iowa: BCO after 1941. Pre-1941: full access to records. Passive registry. Contact: Department of Human Services, Division of Adult, Children and Family Services, Hoover Bldg., Des Moines, IA 50319. (515) 281-5358.

Kansas: OBC at age eighteen. Active Registry. Contact: Department of Social and Rehabilitative Services, Division of Children and Youth Services, 300 S.W. Oakley, Topeka, KS 66606. (913) 296-2500.

Kentucky: Full access at age eighteen with permission of birth parent. Passive registry. Intermediary. Contact: Department of Social Services, Cabinet for Human Resources, 275 E. Main St., 6th Floor W., Frankfort, KY 40621. (502) 564-2136.

Louisiana: BCO. Passive registry at age twenty-five. Contact: Office of Human Development Adoption Program, P.O. Box 3318, Baton Rouge, LA 70821. (504) 342-4040.

Maine: BCO. Passive registry. Contact: State Reunion Registry, c/o Vital Statistics Agency, Department of Human Services, 221 State St., State House, Station 11, Augusta, ME 04333. (207) 289-3184.

Maryland: BCO after June 1, 1947. Pre-1947: OBC with identifying information removed, via intermediary. Contact: Department of Human Resources, 311 W. Saratoga St., Baltimore, MD 21201. (410) 333-0235.

Massachusetts: BCO. Waiver system. Contact: Department of Social Services, 150 Causeway St., Boston, MA 02114. (617) 727-0900.

Michigan: BCO. Waiver system in central registry. Intermediary. Contact: Department of Social Services, P.O. Box 30037, Lansing, MI 48909. (517) 373-3513.

Minnesota: Active Registry. Waiver. Post-1982 placement records released to the adult adoptee unless birth parents have filed a disclosure veto. Contact: Department of Human Services, 444 Lafayette Rd., St. Paul, MN 55155. (612) 296-0584.

Mississippi: BCO. Intermediary. Post-1994; birth parent registry. Contact: Department of Public Welfare, 955 S. Plaza Dr., Jackson, MS 39284. (601) 373-3526.

Missouri: BCO. Active registry requires signature of adoptive parents on adoptions prior to 1986. Contact: Department of Social

Services, Division of Family Services, P.O. Box 88, Jefferson City, MO 65103. (314) 751-2981.

Montana: OBC on adoptions prior to 1967, 1967–1997: BCO. After October 1, 1997: placement records released unless birth parent veto received. Passive registry. Intermediary. Contact: Department of Social and Rehabilitative Services, Social Services Bureau, 111 Sanders St., Helena, MT 59601. (406) 444-5622.

Nebraska: OBC to adult adoptees over age twenty-five with birth parent consent, provided adoptive parents don't veto. Active registry. Intermediary. Contact: Department of Public Welfare, Division of Social Services, P.O. Box 95026, Lincoln, NE 68509. (401) 471-3121.

Nevada: BCO. Passive registry. Contact: Department of Human Resources, Welfare Division, 251 Jeanell Dr., Capitol Mall Complex, Carson City, NV 89710. (702) 687-4760.

New Hampshire: BCO. Waiver system. Intermediary via agency. Contact: Department of Health and Welfare, Bureau of Child and Family Services, 6 Hazen Drive, Concord, NH 03301. (603) 271-6202.

New Jersey: BCO (no provisions). Contact: Department of Institutions and Agencies, Division of Youth and Family Services, P.O. Box 510, Trenton, NJ 08625. (609) 292-8816.

New Mexico: BCO. Intermediary. Contact: Department of Human Services, Adoption Services, P.O. Box 2348, Santa Fe, NM 97504. (505) 827-8413.

New York: BCO. Passive registry, also open to siblings. Contact: New York State Adoption Services, 40 N. Pearl St., Albany, NY 12243. (518) 474-2868. Note: State Reunion Registry can be reacted at N.Y. State Health Department, Adoption Information Registry, Corning Tower, Room 208, Empire State Plaza, Albany, NY 12237. (518) 474-1746.

North Carolina: BCO (no provisions). Contact: Department of Human Resources, Division of Social Services, 325 N. Salisbury, Raleigh, NC 27611. (919) 733-0598.

North Dakota: BCO. Active registry. Waiver. Contact: Department of Children and Family Services, Russell Bldg., P.O. Box 7, Bismarck, ND 58505. (701) 224-2316.

Ohio: BCO on births after 1964. OBC may be obtained on births prior to 1964, unless the adoptive birth certificate was requested for reissue. Passive registry. Registry contact: Vital Statistics Agency, Ohio Department of Health, Division of Vital Statistics, 65 South Front

Street, Columbus, OH 43266, (614) 466-2531. Other queries contact: Department of Human Services, Bureau of Child Services, 30 E. Broad St, 30th Floor, Columbus, OH 43215. (614) 464-4000.

Oklahoma: BCO. Passive registry. Intermediary. Contact: Department of Human Services, Division of Child Welfare, P.O. Box 25352, Oklahoma City, OK 73125. (405) 521-2778.

Oregon: OBC at age twenty-one. Contact Preference. Intermediary. Contact: Department of Human Resources, Adoption Services, 198 Commercial St., S.E., Salem, OR 97310. (503) 378-6224.

Pennsylvania: OBC at age eighteen with waiver from birth parent. Birth parent passive registry. Intermediary. Medical information update registry. Contact: Department of Public Welfare, Office of Children, Youth and Families, P.O. Box 2675, Harrisburg, PA 17120. (717) 787-7750.

Rhode Island: BCO. Passive registry. Contact: Department of Children and Their Families, 618 Mt. Pleasant Ave., Providence, RI 02908. (401) 457-4708.

South Carolina: BCO. Passive registry. Contact: Department of Social Services, Adoption and Birth Parent Services, P.O. Box 1520, Columbia, SC 29202. (803) 734-6095.

South Dakota: BCO. Passive registry. Contact: Department of Social Services, Richard F. Kneip Bldg., 700 Governor's Dr., Pierre, SD 57501. (605) 773-3521.

Tennessee: OBC at age twenty-one unless birth was result of rape or incest. Contact veto. Contact: Department of Human Services, Post Adoption Branch, 400 Deaderick St., Nashville, TN 37248. (615) 741-3263.

Texas: BCO. Passive registry. Contact: State Reunion Registry, Department of Health, Bureau of Vital Statistics, 1100 W. 49th St., Austin, TX 78756. (512) 458-7111.

Utah: BCO. Passive registry. Contact: Adoption Registry, Vital Statistics Agency, P.O. Box 16700, Salt Lake City, UT 84116. (801) 538-6380.

Vermont: Pre-1986: access for adoptees with birth parent consent. Post-1986: access unless a birth parent disclosure veto is filed. Central registry. Waiver. Contact: Department of Social and Rehabilitative Services, 103 S. Main St., Waterbury, VT 05676. (802) 864-7467.

Virginia: BCO on births prior to July 1994. Post-July 1994: OBC at age eighteen with birth parent consent. Intermediary. Contact:

Department of Health, Division of Social Services Adoption Reports Unit, 8007 Discovery Dr., Richmond, VA 23229. (804) 662-9855.

Washington: BCO on births prior to October 1, 1993; OBC at age eighteen after 1993, unless birth parent files a veto. Intermediary. Contact: Department of Social and Health Services: Bureau of Children's Services, Office Building #2, Olympia, WA 98504. (206) 753-7039.

West Virginia: BCO. Passive registry. Contact: Department of Social Services, Adoption Department, 1900 Washington St. E., Charleston, WV 25305. (304) 348-4098.

Wisconsin: OBC at age eighteen with restrictions. Adoptees active registry; birth parent passive registry. Contact: Department of Health and Social Services, Division of Community Services, Attn.: Adoption Search Coordinator, 1 W. Wilson St., Madison, WI 54702. (608) 266-7163.

Wyoming: BCO. Passive registry. Intermediary. Contact: Department of Health and Social Services, Adoption Department, Hathaway Bldg., Cheyenne, WY 82002. (307) 777-7656.

Due to the intricacies and restrictions involved with some of the states offering original birth certificates and/or registries, it is advised that you call or write to your state to obtain specific information and details regarding the filing application process and current assessment fees. The adoption reform movement is active in every state where records remain closed, so legislation may either be pending or recently passed in your state of birth/relinquishment. It is to your benefit to contact the state agency involved with your adoption placement to learn about current events in adoption legislation. We accept no liability for outdated information provided above.

Chapter **11**

An Introduction to the Legal Issues of Reform

As the reform of adoption laws makes its long, slow progress, a recurring theme arises. People searching for their relatives lost through adoption ask, "Why do our laws seem to discourage reunions? Why can't we just get the laws changed so all of the adoption records are opened?"

What seems to be such a logical course of action, however, isn't always immediately attainable. The result of intense efforts by many individuals brings about reform on any issue. In fact, more often than not, the most logical solutions are the ones most difficult to obtain. The issue of open adoption records is no exception.

Conflicts in Open Records

The term "open records" doesn't even have a clear definition. Adoption triad members are often conflicted about the intent of open records, which makes it difficult to agree upon and even more difficult for the general public to understand. To most adoptees, birth parents and adoptive parents, "open records" is simply this: The records surrounding the legal process of an adoption are open and accessible (not sealed), and they identify the biological relations by name.

Activist Groups Take Different Approaches

Because the activism scene includes people with a wide range of goals, it may help you to know who's out there advocating for adoption reform. Traditional adoption reform advocates like the American Adoption Congress (AAC) and Concerned United Birthparents (CUB) have taken the road to open records one step at a time, accepting passive or active reunion registries on the theory that something is better than nothing. Many open records advocates have been in battle with the legislative system for more than twenty years. They have firsthand experience with the politics involved, as well as the barrage of barriers presented with each new proposed legislation (stalling tactics, for example). As years go by, and no acceptable open adoption records legislation is passed, many advocates feel that some level of compromise is necessary "To accept something—even a passive registry—might benefit some of our people. The inability to compromise might keep even the small numbers of passive registry users from ever experiencing a reunion," one reformist with the AAC explained.

At the other end of the spectrum, a relatively new organization on the adoption reform scene, Bastard Nation (BN), has expanded the definition of the term "open records." Advocates within BN define open records as including access to the original birth certificate. Currently, while records might be opened to an adoptee or birth parent case by case or even state by state, the opened record does not necessarily include the original birth certificate.

It has taken the voice of this young, outspoken organization to make adoption reformists take a harder look at their own missions and intent for adoption legislation. Bastard Nation takes an unbending stand that closed records are a violation of civil rights for the adoptee, and this position has created conflict within the reform community. While all adoption activists believe that closed records violate the civil rights of adoptees, controversy exists when it comes to compromising on open records legislation.

Both BN and AAC leaders continue to fight for open records. BN zealously forges ahead to win access to original birth certificates on demand for every adoptee. The AAC is a bit more conservative due to the frustrations of their past lobbying efforts. Although their members would be thrilled with open access to original birth certificates across the nation, they have been willing to support any move toward open records, including passive or active reunion registries, or open records that include contact vetoes.

Dynamics of the Contact Veto

Contact vetoes are relatively new in adoption legislation. The contact veto allows a birth parent or adoptee the right to prevent the other one from learning their identity by filing a disclaimer, which prohibits direct contact. This provision allows the searching person access to updated medical information, but does not include the identity of the person being sought.

When a state opens its adoption records by legislative or referendum vote with a contact veto amendment attached, the provision includes a set period of time, usually one year, during which adoptees and birth parents who wish their identities to remain private can file a contact veto disclaimer. After the legal deadline passes, the adoption records are open and information can be exchanged, except for information covered by the contact veto. This provides a method for the exchange of information while protecting the other individual's right to privacy.

Advocates of the contact veto believe this compromise provides the rudimentary elements of open records without breaching confidentiality for either party involved. But at the 2000 AAC Conference, we heard a variety of interesting arguments against the provision of contact vetoes in open records legislation, including:

- The adoptee is no longer a minor child needing protection, but is now an adult and should have full access to information about his biological heritage, as is provided to any nonadopted person under the Freedom of Information Act.

- The birth parents' "right to privacy" is not included in any legal documentation. It is merely implied by the nature of adoption, and should have no legal bearing on an adoptee's "right to know."

- The adoptee's rights supersede any promises made to birth parents.

- To refuse an adoptee access to his original birth certificate is a form of discrimination and is therefore unconstitutional.

- The issue isn't reunion, but rather the right to have access to our own information.

Of course, contact vetoes can be more complicated and detailed than we are able to explain here, but we hope this simplified explanation gives you a basic understanding of the issues at hand.

Regardless of the varying methods of approach, the AAC and BN, as well as many other national, state, and local organizations yet unmentioned, are actively working for open records in adoption. So, whose methods are right? The answer ultimately depends upon whom you ask, and we certainly aren't looking to start further controversy between adoption triad members. Both the AAC and BN are

vital to reform, and we support both of them. We believe it is important for citizens to support open records in whatever form best suits
their comfort level.

Obstacles in Activism

The National Council For Adoption (NCFA), the American Center
for Law and Justice (ACLJ), and the Christian Coalition, the major
organizations that oppose open records, have succeeded in raising
support to maintain sealed records. One wonders why, since a significant number of people want to know more about their genetic roots.

Why haven't we seen more of an outpouring of protesters
demanding reform in adoption? There are a number of possible
reasons:

- Unity and cohesiveness within the adoption reform movement haven't been consistent enough to educate and rally
  support among the masses.

- There aren't enough financial or physical resources within
  the adoption reform movement to lobby effectively

- It's easier for legislators to support the status quo than to
  expend time and energy attempting to understand what
  they perceive to be the complexities of open records—or to
  get caught up in the controversies surrounding adoption
  reform.

- Proponents of closed records have secured the financial
  resources needed to lobby against open records.

- Secrecy is more easily accepted by the people in power.

- The adoption reform movement lacks harmony in its call to
  activism.

As you can see, the issues surrounding the reform movement
are anything but clear-cut. To further complicate matters, the goals of
adoption-reform advocates are wide-ranging. For example, there are
several identifiable classifications of idealists including, but not limited to those who:

- Will accept nothing less than original birth certificates

- Will accept anything that leads toward the exchange of
  identifying information

- Believe a birth mother's identity should remain confidential

- Believe adoptees should be allowed identifying information about their birth parents, but the birth parents should get no information unless the adoptee makes contact with them

- Support the perceived protection closed records provide

- Believe open records in adoption should be granted only on a case-by-case basis of medical need

- Believe *all* adoption records should be *open*, forcing birth parents and adoptive parents to petition the courts to get the records closed by proving "just cause" for such an action

Put yourself in the position of your legislator and ask, "Which constituents have presented me with the clearest, most concise understanding of their needs?" Would you vote yes or no for open record legislation? What influencing factors sway your vote? If you are in hearings listening to testimony from both sides, would you vote in support of the side that presented different perspectives on the same view, or would you vote in support of the side that made unified presentations from the same perspective?

Do you vote "yes" on an issue you aren't clear about, or do you vote "no" in support of current laws? Do you vote for the complicated argument or the easy-to-understand one? So far, regardless of the underlying factors, most legislators choose to vote in support of current laws.

The Silent Majority

Birth mothers haven't been as active in reform as adoptees, except as a "silent majority." This doesn't mean they don't believe in the sacredness and necessity of adoption reunions, considering that it's estimated that 98 percent of birth mothers would welcome the opportunity for a reunion (Giddens 1998).

There are varied reasons as to why birth mothers aren't particularly prominent in the activism sphere: Shame. Fear. Low self-esteem. Uncertainty as to their "rights" or place pertaining to their relinquished birth child's life. The stigma associated with being a birth mother prevents many of them from being able to go public. While understandable, this is also unfortunate. Too many opponents of open adoption records take advantage of the silence birth mothers maintain and claim to speak for them, demanding that records remain closed in an effort to protect the birth mother's privacy.

Speculation and Cynicism in Reform

Many accusations have been made about lawmakers who don't support open records, and you've probably heard most of them. Some advocates suggest that our legislators fear open records because there are "too many birth parents in politics." Other advocates have accused lawmakers of being "in the pockets of the NCFA," "adoptive parents who don't want birth mothers ringing their doorbells, asking to see their children," or simply fearful of the unknown.

Because most people are cynical about politics, triad members often question the integrity of lawmakers when the voting results are against opening sealed records. We tend to wonder, "Exactly what is it they are trying to hide?" or "What are their ulterior motives?"

To open records advocates, opening adoption records seems like a logical, sensible, moral initiative. To closed records advocates, opening sealed records is a simple violation of the law and a breach of confidentiality for the people the laws were written to protect.

Advocating Your Rights

Here's something to keep in mind when advocating for adoption reform: raising empathy for your issue is crucial in garnering support.

Familiarize yourself with your legislative representatives. Ask them questions. Learn if they are adopted, an adoptive or birth parent, or even a friend of a triad member. Share your personal story with them. Be precise about what you want to see in adoption reform and ask them for support. You pay their salaries with your tax dollars, so don't be too shy or embarrassed to question their position on any issue that's important to you.

Until our legislators are educated about the deepest and most sensitive issues of adoption, they won't be motivated to support much beyond what currently exists in their state for adoption laws. They haven't been overwhelmingly convinced that adoption reunions are emotionally healthy and necessary, and opponents have done a better job in convincing them to keep the current closed laws.

Interestingly, reform advocates with less experience working with legislators have been critical toward what they perceive as the "old regime." With so little accomplished, reform rookies convince themselves that some leaf has been either left unturned, some approach hasn't been tried, or something wasn't done "right," which is an unfair and inaccurate assessment.

Right or wrong methods aside, any individual or group who has heeded the call of open adoption reform is to be commended. Nothing is easy when it comes to changing laws. Patience and fortitude are essential, as is being able to maintain a good sense of humor. If you can't stop and laugh at yourself and the situation occasionally, activism might drive a sane person mad.

Chapter 12

Sojourn of Entanglement

Over the decades, society has seemingly viewed adoption as a rather black-and-white, simple concept: A teenage girl becomes pregnant out of wedlock and surrenders the baby for adoption. The psychology of coercion doesn't typically enter anyone's mind because of the socially accepted myth that relinquishment was a *choice* made by the birth mother.

Society perpetuates this myth, and our legal system creates laws in support of it. Relinquishment papers, which are nothing more than contractual agreements, are written to deliberately alienate the birth mother/father and protect the adoptive parents. The child, regardless of the good intentions of all parties, is reduced to being a negotiated commodity.

It's not unusual for companies to break or amend contracts after the fact or look for loopholes. However, in adoption, when a birth parent decides to challenge the legal contract, it often becomes a media event, causing folks to emotionally take sides with one of the two parties. This is just one more example of our double-edged system of justice and social acceptance. Most of us tend to ignore the typical business transactions, even those that might affect thousands of people, like company takeovers, factory and store closings, or other rules of corporate engagement. But if a birth mother or father changes their mind about an adoption contract and the media gets wind of the news, it's often used as propaganda against birth parents. Attempting to nullify an adoption contract becomes an issue tried in the media, with fingers being pointed by everyone involved and nobody truly able to look after the best interest of the child because of all the interference.

Sadly, with the exception of the child, who can't speak for himself, everyone involved in the adoption process genuinely believes that their motives are altruistic and that the best interests of the child *are* being served. In reality, however, the only interests served are those who have the most to gain: the adoptive parents who want a child; the adoption agency who collects a fee; and to a degree, the birth parents who have been convinced that relinquishment is their only hope either to have a second chance at life or to be relieved of the responsibility of parenting while still knowing that their child will be cared for (or, in the case of their attempt to rescind the adoption contract, their gain would be the return of their child).

Although the adoption process should raise eyebrows and questions, it doesn't; at least not on the massive scale that might actually make a difference in current practice. We are a society of contradictions, and that includes our accepted views on adoption. If, as a society, we were truly intent on preserving the "best interest of the child," then we should push lawmakers to include a reunion plan within every adoption contract.

We can't continue to ask a birth mother to release her child for adoption just because she isn't married and then accuse her of being a bad person for giving up her own flesh and blood. We shouldn't promise her that relinquishment is in the best interest of the child while our court system continues to rule that a child's place is with his natural mother. But it's done in America every day. Mixed messages about adoption have existed for generations.

So, how do we change this system of conflicting messages? One solution might be to plant seeds within adoption contracts that actually provide for the child's best interest when he reaches adulthood and allow him to grow up, rather than always be the proverbial infant in adoption. In our opinion, an alternative that would be in the best interest of the child would be to include provisions for reunion within the initial adoption contract. This would guarantee both the adoptee and the birth parents a legal process to seek out one another under mutual consent when the adoptee reaches the age of majority, without conflict or contradiction from the state government, the originating agency of record, the adoptive parents, or society in general. It's a novel idea that we hope will someday soon be championed by activists and entered into legislation everywhere by our lawmakers.

Reunions in Relation to Open Records

In writing this book, we have tried to stick to the single issue of reunion and found it an impossible task. Reunion, while arguably having little or no bearing on open records, is undeniably its by-product, and there is no way to get around it.

Organizations legislating for open records believe that "Open records is not about reunions. It's about rights." And this is true. However, once information is exchanged and identities disclosed, reunions ultimately will occur.

Our goal in this book isn't to debate issues of open records versus other methods of contact between adoptees and birth family. The information on these pages provides people faced with the opportunity of a reunion a better understanding of the process leading to contact, clarification of the issues they might face, and food for thought in making their own informed choices as they move through reunion. Our personal opinions have been clearly expressed throughout this text. We believe in and support efforts that lead to fulfilling an adoptee's right to his original birth certificate and all recorded information surrounding his birth.

The reason open records are important to the reunion process is because without them, fewer reunions are possible. As long as records remain closed, the person seeking a reunion is forced to circumvent their state legal system one way or another, even if only by registering with a voluntary mutual consent reunion registry not funded by their state.

Will keeping adoption records sealed prevent reunions? In many cases the answer is "yes." Sealed adoption records prevent reunions from occurring for people who don't have the financial resources to hire a private investigator; or the wherewithal to lie; or the courage to demand; or the knowledge to petition or find some other legal loophole; or the patience to sustain the search for the many years it might take. Open records provide direct access to the information needed for reunions to occur.

Will opening adoption records prevent you from experiencing the emotional turmoil so many adoptees and birth mothers talk about? No. Reunions are filled with emotions, and an open adoption record will not numb you to your own emotions. It may, however, save you many years of search and the emotional stress associated with the search process. Open records can lead you directly into your reunion, or at the least, give you the information you seek about your biological family.

Make no mistake: Open records do not always result in reunion. You can have one without the other. Just because your state opens its adoption records doesn't mean you must be forced into a reunion. Open records provide you with choices that the state did not previously allow you to have. After you receive your adoption records, you can decide whether or not you want to find the person or persons named on the documents. The decision is yours.

Of course, some states with open records may also have implemented a disclosure system of some sort, such as contact veto, contact preference, or waivers (defined in the previous chapter). If you live in an open records state, you should refer to their provisions to learn which, if any, of these systems is in place. A fine or other deterrent might be attached to the contact veto if you make contact beyond the disclaimer. This gives rise to another question and argument:

Will a contact veto or contact preference keep a person from having a reunion with their biological family? Admittedly, it won't. Penalties for violating a contact disclosure are not severe enough to be a deterrent for people who are intent on meeting their birth parents or relinquished child. However, it is believed that most people will respect the privacy and rights of the other person and each party will operate with a high level of integrity.

Let's face it. Once you have your information in hand and you know the other person is not emotionally able to handle meeting you in person, would you really want to force your way into their life? Or would you respect their wishes, be satisfied with the information you received, and move on with your life? Despite the pessimism expressed by those against open records, and the lack of faith they have in both the system and mankind's ability to operate with integrity, we believe the overwhelming majority of participants will adhere to the policy's restrictions.

A certain level of emotion surrounding rejection at birth already exists in adoption. Learning about a contact disclosure filed in your records might expose you to a new set of emotions. You might feel rejected for a second time, and even angry. These feelings shouldn't be denied, but rather embraced, in an effort to understand the severity of the issues remaining locked within the other person. This may also help you accept the knowledge you have gained, then move on with your life.

Sometimes in life, no matter how much we want the answer to be "yes," it will be "no." If your quest for a reunion with your birth kin has brought you identities you never before knew and information you only dreamed about, then you have achieved something special, regardless of whether you had a reunion with the person you were seeking.

How Do People Have Reunions in States Where Records Are Closed?

Finding birth family in a state with sealed adoption records is often the result of sheer luck and determination. Word of success in searches spreads like wildfire among adoptees and birth mothers, so successful methods are passed along for other searchers to try.

People in closed records states are often reluctant to publicly share the how-to's of their search success, for fear of legal ramifications. For example, during subcommittee hearings on adoption reform in North Carolina a few years ago, the Legislative Review Committee (LRC) listened to an adoptee who presented testimony that included the touching reunion story of finally meeting her birth mother. When directly questioned by a senator on the panel as to just how she found her birth mother, the young woman politely described her diligence in researching public records.

"I felt like I had been put in the hot seat," she said. "I know records are closed here, so I didn't know how much to tell them. I didn't want to get anybody in trouble for having helped me, and at the same time I wanted to shout it from the rooftop because without help, I never would have found her."

The intimidation this adoptee felt is understandable. However, she did nothing illegal. She had been given her nonidentifying information, which is allowed by law, and proceeded with her search, using advice from another person with experience at searching through public records to find people. She was able to locate her birth mother by a step-by-step process of elimination.

Your nonidentifying information can sometimes be the essential link in your search. These are some of the details you might expect to find:

- Ages of the birth mother and father at the time of the birth

- The birth parents' student status, academic standing, and class involvement, as well as type of employment

- Hair and eye color of the birth parents, as well as build and nationality

- Hobbies, interests, and talents of the birth parents

- Medical history of birth parents and birth grandparents at the time the adoptee was born

- Profession of the maternal and/or paternal grandparents

- Birth grandparents' political affiliation and socioeconomic background information

Sometimes, however, information is not as detailed as this—it may be sketchy at best. There are no universal or standard guidelines on the type or amount of details contained in nonidentifying information, so it is left entirely to the discretion and interpretation of the agency, county, or state involved in the adoption.

When information is as detailed as that listed above, the narrowing process is easier. Looking through public records, such as land deeds, voter registration, newspapers, school yearbooks, etc., you can match noteworthy characteristics while eliminating others. Of course, if you receive very ambiguous nonidentifying information, it makes search more difficult.

However, it's important to realize that some people who receive detailed nonidentifying information can have just as difficult a time finding their biological relatives as the person who receives vague information. There is no formula for success in the process of search and reunion. Trial and error are the ruling factors, and your own flexibility, acceptance, patience, and emotions play crucial roles as well. A list of books that you might find helpful as guides in your search are included in the Suggested Reading section of this book.

When the Legal System Fails

Until adoption records are opened in every state, there will always be room for the legal system to fail on one level or another. While that isn't fair, particularly in states that have a mechanism in place for reunion, it is reality. Any time human hands are involved in a process, a potential exists for error. Even in states that provide a mechanism to promote reunions, you might see lengthy delays in processing the requested information, disbursement of incorrect information, and/or a lack of general follow-through.

The complaint most often expressed by adoptees and birth parents (primarily birth mothers) involves the system's inability to exchange information between the adoptee and birth parent, despite mutual consent. It can be exceptionally frustrating when both parties express a desire to meet, but agencies are forbidden by law from releasing identifying information.

"I sent a letter to Children's Home Society when I began my search five years ago," said Cindy, a birth mother. "I asked them to place the letter in my daughter's folder in case she ever contacted them wanting more information about me. I was in remission with breast cancer and thought it was important that she have an updated medical history."

After Cindy met her daughter, Laura, they discovered that they had both sent similar letters, authorizing the agency to provide information to the other upon request. Laura had mailed hers a year prior to Cindy's letter, so they were both surprised to learn that the agency didn't follow through with their request to exchange information. In fact, their reunion wasn't the result of a connection made via the agency—Cindy hired a private investigator to locate Laura.

The reason that Cindy and Laura never received each other's letters was due to their state's position on sealed records. "It's frustrating for us, as the agency, to have both letters sitting in the same folder and the law says we cannot forward them to the individuals involved," explained an employee of Children's Home Society.

But to Laura and Cindy, it made no sense to withhold information from two adults who desire a reunion and have clearly indicated their intentions in writing with their agency. "We didn't ask anybody to search for us. We each wrote a letter asking the agency to give it to the other one if any interest or request for information was expressed. All they had to do after receiving the second letter was deliver them to each of us. That would have saved us both years of searching and several thousand dollars," Cindy said with frustration.

Laura agreed. "The system is definitely flawed. I just thank God that my mom's breast cancer was in remission and nothing worse had happened before we were reunited. I can't begin to imagine what I would have done if I had found that she passed away from the cancer and we had each written letters to the agency permitting an exchange of information."

The Journey of a Mother and Son

Whitney, now a middle-aged adult, searched for her son for several years. She also sent letters to her agency expressing a desire for reunion with her son and giving her permission for the agency to release her identifying information to him if he ever requested it. She wrote the following about her experience and the meeting with her son, Tom.

When I was young, I relinquished my baby son for adoption through the Children's Home Society. When he turned twenty-one, I began to search for him by signing up in various private registries. The agency allowed me to place a letter to my son in his file, in the event he ever requested information about me. My six-page letter told him all about my family and me, his biological father (who supported this effort, as did my dear husband), and the desire and willingness of all of us to know him and help him in any way he might need.

I continued my search for years, but with no success. Finally, my husband and I hired a private investigator because I had begun to feel a sense of concern and urgency. The investigator called two weeks later, with this stunningly short report: "We have found your son; he is dead. He died of AIDS last year at the age of twenty-seven."

About eighteen months before he died, my son had written to the agency asking for information about me, but they were unable to tell him anything other than nondescript information about my height, coloring, and the medical condition of family members. They apparently felt they could not give him my letter because of the law forbidding them to release identifying information.

When my son contacted the agency, he was twenty-six years old. He had been diagnosed with HIV on his twenty-first birthday and was dying. As his friends have since told me, he had no access to a computer and so could not sign up for the registries available on the Internet. The first and only registry he called advised him that he would first have to pay a $2,700 fee, and he gave up. And then he went to his grave, never knowing.

He was, from what I see on a video of him, delightful. His IQ was 180; he was a composer, pianist, and trumpeter; he wrote beautifully; he was guileless, kind, generous, and well loved by his friends. He wanted to become an Episcopal priest, but was turned down from the seminary because he had AIDS. He was candid about having AIDS and assiduously careful never to pass on to another person this dreadful disease, which was inflicted on him when he was attacked while hitchhiking. He and his parents had withdrawn from one another.

Oh, if only we could have known, and gone to him, and given him help, or told him the story of why he was given up for adoption and how this was done with a heavy heart, but in the honest belief that it was the best way to love him—to let him have two parents and a stable home.

When I gave my baby up, I felt that I was in a burning building handing him to safety. I thought he would always know that this was an act of love. But judging now from the things he said and wrote, he never believed this. My first realization of this possibility came before I found him, when I read a book by Tim Green, the NFL football player, who was adopted. He wrote that children do not see their adoption as we wish them to. They see things more simply, more intuitively: People who love you want to be with you and, therefore, I was given away because I was not loved and was, in fact, unlovable. I learned from my son's friends that my son anguished over who we were and why we did not keep him or care for him.

Some say that confidentiality is necessary to protect birth parents, but it was never my understanding that I would be shielded from my son or his questions. If I had thought the state would make it impossible for him to find me, I'm not sure I'd

*have been able to go through with the adoption. It was always a
dream of mine, and the other girls I knew in the unwed mother's
home, that when our children were grown they would be able to
contact us.*

*We fortunate ones who know our families can talk about
how we look like our grandparents, have the same interests as
our dad, or talk like our mom. This piece of jewelry or furniture
belonged to my great-grandmother. This is my aunt's recipe.
This set of encyclopedias was my father's. I remind my family
of one of our ancestors in the way I twist my forelock or walk
with a certain gait, or have the same sense of humor or laugh
or temperament.*

*We know these things, or with a little digging, can find
out. This is our birthright. We cannot just leave our relinquished
children in the fog, groping on into adulthood for a sense of who
they are, wondering whether they were loved.*

The Synchronous Journey

One of the greatest joys of reunion is discovering the reality of a connection between the two of you. It is a connection that is often indescribable to its participants and hardly believable by those who hear
their experiences. These are the stories that cause us to recognize the
powers of the universe.

The "synchronous journey" begins like a dream held tightly
within the heart. It begins as a wish and, over the years, grows into
the hope of reunion. As time goes on, the birth mother is able to
identify with every child she sees who might be the same age as the
one she relinquished. Are you my child, she wonders? Could you
be?

In her book, *Synchronicity and Adoption: The Genetic Connection of
Adoptees and Birthparents* (1992), author LaVonne Harper Stiffler
noted interesting events between adoptees and birthparents that are
considered to be more than mere coincidence.

"Like the migratory and homing behaviors of animals, which
have been known, admired, expected, yet mysterious to mankind of
all generations, parent-child reunions have an element of awe. After
their initial contact, families begin to talk about the intricacies of the
search process, and many are astonished by the synchronicities of location and timing that led them to each other. In my initial study of sev-
enty families, nine of them had intersection in location during search,
and twenty-three had coincidences in the timing of their search."

Some of the amazing coincidences, or synchronicities, cited by
Stiffler include: "Two searching adoptees were drawn to timely

encounters with judges who unexpectedly opened records for them; four persons were approached by strangers who offered surprising information. A mother and daughter began working at the same store within days of each other. Another mother reached her son just before his planned move to a distant country. Members of four families began to make inquiries in a search for one another at the same time (within days or weeks)." (p. 43)

We have heard many similar tales from reunited adoptees and birth mothers to support Stiffler's observations. Theresa, a birth mother, found her son, Michael, within one week of deciding to search for him. Out of dire curiosity, she and her husband drove to Michael's and sat outside his house for a while, overcome with awe for having such incredible "luck."

After checking into a local hotel, she called Michael and nervously introduced herself. He was completely receptive to meeting her. Within a week of beginning her search, Theresa had her arms wrapped around Michael in a welcome, warm embrace for the second time in twenty-seven years. Michael confided that he had recently been trying to begin his search for her. He had wanted to find her for several years, and in recent weeks, she had suddenly been intensely on his mind. Both of Michael's adoptive parents had passed away, which led him to think about his birth mother a great deal.

As the two talked through the events of their lives, which included numerous moves back and forth across the country, they learned they had both lived in or near the same towns on three occasions.

The more reunions that take place despite the legal system, the more stories are shared about these synchronous journeys between adoptees and birth parents. Even Whitney, who still deals with issues of loss concerning the death of her son, Tom, recognizes the momentous coincidences that occurred between them.

Following their graveside reunion, Whitney was able to forge a relationship with some of her son's friends. It was through them and their adoration for Tom that Whitney came to know the beauty of her son and realize how their paths crossed on both a spiritual and literal level.

Tom was an incredibly sensitive and talented person. Whitney was told that Tom used to recall the pangs of his birth in detail. He told people that he actually had memories of being born. Through his journal, he was able to express some of his emotions surrounding his birth, his adoption, his life as an adoptee, his birth family and his illness. The journal was given to Whitney by Tom's friends, and a portion of it is reprinted below with her permission.

On September 3, 1997, Tom lay dying in a two-room apartment in Boone, North Carolina. While Tom was being held by his friends, his birth mother, Whitney, unknowingly wandered the streets of the same city, within steps of her son. Tom wrote:

> *I pray my death may be the best death for this self*
> *I pray that my life be wonderful and peaceful*
> *I pray that I may walk in the best light*
> > *The highest light*
> > *And that I remember*
> > *HIV is my child*
> > *And NOT the thing to contend with*
> > *But instead to nurture.*
>
> *My mother contended with me—*
> > *Out of ignorance and youthfulness.*
>
> *I know better.*
> *I will not do the same.*
>
> *The rock I sit on is cool*
> > *The sun is warm*
> > *The air . . . perfect*
> > *The fear . . . lessened*
> > *The water . . . burbling.*
>
> > > *Perhaps not quite peace*
> > > *But close enough.*
> > > > —Tom L.

Whitney and Tom were victims of a system committed to preventing reunions. Sadly, theirs is not an isolated story. Thousands of adoptees and birth parents in America will die waiting for their reunions. The extremity of stories such as Whitney and Tom's forces us to take a good, hard look at our current closed record system. These two people clearly wanted a reunion. Their letters were on file with their agency, but no one had the courage to do the right thing and forward their letters to one another. Agency policy said "no." The law said "no." It is up to us to work toward the day when "yes" is the unanimous answer.

Do Open Adoption Records Increase Abortion Rates?

The road to opening adoption records has been plagued with bitter argument. We hope we've given you a complete picture of the argument for open records. Those who support sealed records most often argue that they wish to protect the confidentiality of the birth mother. However, despite the data from open records states, some closed-records advocates claim that open records would result in increased abortion rates because some women would rather have an abortion than leave open the possibility that their child might track them down one day.

Birth mothers are assured that their relinquishment is a true sign of love for their child. They entrust their most precious possession to strangers based on faith, either in a higher power or in humanity, and one would hope that adoptive parents operate on the same principle. To suggest that birth mothers would rather have an abortion than to have their identity revealed to their biological child isn't merely misleading, it's completely untrue. There is no research to support these claims, but there has been research to support the opposite claim: Adoption rates increase in states where records are completely open, and abortion rates decrease.

Adoption vs. Abortion: One Woman's Story

Marilyn had relinquished her newborn son to adoption just eighteen months prior to learning that she was pregnant with a second child. She explained that her decision to have an abortion was directly based on her experience with relinquishment.

"I was still traumatized over having lost my son, with no hope of seeing him or knowing anything about him. It was torture. I felt beaten again, and there was no way I was going to give up another baby to adoption.

"That's why I chose abortion. Having given up my first baby to adoption, never knowing how he was doing, if he was happy, if I had made the right decision for him; that's something I knew I couldn't get over again. His was the life I felt growing and kicking inside me. He was the one I loved and came to know."

Marilyn finds the argument of abortion used by opponents of open records to be nothing more than statements made out of ignorance as a ruse to confuse the issue of open records. As a strong advocate for open records, she has met many birth mothers. "They come from all different social and economic backgrounds with varying levels of education, and yet, we share this common thread of relinquishment that seems to bind us all together in solidarity, despite our apparent differences. You would think that a birth mother who is sensitive and concerned about the happiness and welfare of the child she relinquished, as demonstrated by her desire to have information about that child, would earn the respect of adoptive parents and society. But that still doesn't happen. Society still views birth mothers as 'bad,' birth fathers as 'sowing their wild seeds,' adoptive parents as 'saviors or saints,' adoptees as 'children who need to be protected,' and adoptees who search for their birth families as 'ungrateful children.' Reality has very little to do with adoption. There's something terribly wrong here."

Sentiments similar to Marilyn's have been expressed across the country by birth mothers, adoptees, adoptive parents, and others who support open records in adoption that ultimately lead to reunions.

Part **4**

More Help for
Your Journey

Epilogue

Your reunion actually begins the day you decide to search. Regardless of your reason for searching, whether it's for medical need, idle curiosity, or a yearning to know more about yourself—even if you say you have "no intention of meeting the other person"— you have begun a mental journey toward reunion.

From the first moment you begin thinking about finding someone lost to you through adoption, your mind will flood with speculation, hope, dreams, and fantasies, wondering if, when, how, and what it will be like to meet that other person. This is the nature of the reunion beast and there's absolutely no way to travel the reunion path without experiencing all of its detours and forks in the road.

Your quest for reunion might be a very long journey. You might never achieve reunion, or it could occur mere days after your search begins. It might lead you in directions you had never before allowed yourself to imagine, as it did for the people whose stories are contained in these pages.

As one of the most personal journeys a person can make, reunion is naturally filled with emotions and speculation. Adoptees in search might for the first time in their lives be able to relate, if only partially, to the terribly difficult their birth mother experienced upon signing relinquishment papers that were expected to separate them for life.

If you use this time wisely, your progress toward reunion will help you work through any personal issues surrounding your birth parents and your adopted status. It's better to resolve as many of these issues as possible before entering a one-on-one reunion. Feelings of anger, rejection, abandonment, ambivalence, and despondence are all normal emotions you might experience as you journey toward reunion. However, if you want to sustain a relationship with the other person it's best to replace these emotions with hope, empathy, acceptance, and possibly forgiveness. Negative emotions are harmful to any relationship, adopted or otherwise.

Birth mothers will experience emotions similar to those of adoptees—but possibly more intense. The prevailing philosophy that "time heals all wounds," which most birth mothers were reassured at relinquishment, is false. Time doesn't heal anything for birth mothers. Instead, it generally serves as a reminder that adoption means loss—and a permanent one at that. A birth mother can never recapture the lost years, even with a reunion. She will also find herself thrown through time, reliving the experience of pregnancy, broken relationships, anger or hard feelings with her family, labor and birth. And finally, she will again confront her grief over having lost something most precious to her, then being told to "bury" the experience deep within her and never divulge its secrets.

For some birth mothers, the emotions are buried deeper than for others. In these cases, a woman might never be in a psychological position to experience reunion. If you are an adoptee and are rejected by your birth mother either at first contact or later in reunion, there will be few words anyone can offer to comfort you. You will feel rejected and abandoned by this woman for a second time in your life.

If you are able to work through your own emotions of rejection, try to put yourself in her position. Your birth mother was conditioned to forget you, and in some cases it was more like brainwashing. She was told that if she "loved you" she would "forget you" so that you could be completely free, emotionally and physically, to bond with your adoptive family. She was told to never tell anyone about having relinquished you for adoption because bad things might happen to her if she did tell.

Although the attempt to forget you never worked because she always held on to memories and fantasies of you, she most likely did keep your existence a secret. If she never told anyone in her immediate family, your contact will be perceived as a threat to all that she has held private and secret for decades.

You can't overcome emotional wounds with one phone call, or one visit, or one letter. For some birth mothers, the wound of relinquishment will always exist. At the least it will be a scar to remind her; at worst the wound gapes open forever, unable to heal. In some of those cases, she will become conscious of her wound and find a way to apply anesthetic to it—the anesthetic being an attempt to discover information about you.

Remember that no two people are exactly alike. You can't expect your birth mother or relinquished child to accept you in reunion as readily as someone else's did. Don't make comparisons and gauge the success or failure of your reunion relationship against another person's. There is no formula for success in reunion, only commonsense guidelines to help you proceed with integrity and honor, regardless of the reunion's outcome.

Some pitfalls to reunion are more obvious than others. Beginning a reunion with demands—even subtle ones or those made in jest—can doom a relationship.

One reunion relationship we know about has had a very difficult time advancing. The birth mother conducted a search for her son, who seemed most receptive to her having found him. She showered him with expensive gifts. Whenever he hinted that he wanted something, she purchased it for him.

He also happened to be in severe financial distress, and the birth mother, feeling a need to make amends and take care of him, loaned him several thousand dollars. Afterwards, she began making demands from him for attention, which escalated until she was trying to force him to live his life by her standards, alienating some of his other relationships. Naturally, he withdrew from her and refused to respond to her demands.

Sadly, she could have avoided these pitfalls if she had controlled her own behavior. She was unable to accept her role as birth mother. She gave into her emotions and moved beyond the proverbial "doting, interfering" mom. She had lived with her fantasies about him since the day he was born and was compelled to become "instant mother" to him, unable to recognize that he had not lived with the same dreams.

Less than two years into the relationship, her son distanced himself to the point of no contact. Still unable to accept her role in the relationship's failure, she projected the problems onto him.

It is vital that both birth mothers and adoptees realize two things: 1) Relationships in general aren't built overnight. This is particularly true of reunion relationships, which develop through a series of stages over time. 2) Although this is the woman who gave birth to you, she is not the mother who raised you. There is a lifetime of familiarity missing between you, and your relationship so far has been built on fantasy.

Once the two of you meet, the fantasy must end and you must begin working on your relationship in the real world. You will need to come to terms very quickly with the fact that nobody is perfect. People are flawed and not built to live up to fantasies.

In the scenario above, it's obvious that the birth mother was attempting to buy her son's affections. With her gifts and money, she was expecting her fantasies to be fulfilled, but she wasn't able to see things in this light. Her son did, though, and he reacted as would be expected by distancing himself from her.

Despite all that occurred between them, it's possible that their relationship can be repaired. The birth mother will need professional help and guidance to understand her behavior and learn from her mistakes. Her son might also benefit from therapy to learn how to deal with his birth mother, as well as how to handle his own behaviors more appropriately so he doesn't lead her on in the future. Either way, it will take time to repair their relationship, and it will also take honesty and open communication. It's a rather sad way to begin a reunion, but sometimes it can't be helped, due to the participants' lack of self-improvement work or simply their personalities.

Many adoption-based reunions develop into lifelong relationships. Either by nature or guidance, these reunion participants manage to avoid the pitfalls that lead to failed relationships. The most successful reunion stories we've heard about are the ones in which an extensive support system was in place. In these success stories, adoptees and birth parents were able to openly communicate with their current family members to let them know their intentions and desires for a reunion. Their families were supportive, and they themselves were active in adoption support groups led by other triad members experienced in the reunion process. When these adoptees and birth parents cried over the frustrations of search, they had people who cried along with them—supporters who knew how they were feeling, or maybe didn't know exactly how they were feeling but were otherwise able to empathize.

Having a support system in place is vital to reunion. While it's helpful if your support team agrees with your intentions and plans, it's even better for you to have supportive friends who remain objective and question you as you move toward reunion. This helps you maintain an objective perspective and modify your course as needed throughout your journey. Just because someone asks you to question your motives, your ideas, and your plans, doesn't mean they aren't being supportive. Consider yourself fortunate if you have someone who will question you along the way.

Find other ways to involve yourself in adoption issues that can bring you a better understanding of and insight into your own issues, as well as empathy toward others. You can learn a great deal by attending adoption conferences and workshops, and it gives you the opportunity to meet other members of the adoption triad, possibly for the first time in your life. Any opportunity to gain better understanding about what you can expect, or about the emotions the person you're seeking might be experiencing, can only help your transition into reunion.

While waiting for information from sources, or while taking a break from your search efforts, consider getting involved in adoption legislation reform, particularly if you live in a closed-records state. Write to your lawmakers and state your position. Ask them to support open-record legislation. Consider becoming an activist in adoption reform. The more people in the public's eye, the better the chance for change.

Release your issues, frustrations, or joys through something creative. The ranks of adoptees and birth parents include some very talented people. In this creative expression, you would be joining a few notable birth parents, including Joni Mitchell, Roseanne, David Crosby, and Hank Williams. Your expression of creativity would also align you with many talented adoptees, including Edward Albee, Ann-Margret, Richard Burton, former president Gerald Ford, James Michener, Dave Thomas, and Melissa Gilbert.

Regrettably, sometimes in life our notoriety is the result of someone else's bad behavior, poor choices, or mental incapacity. Christina Crawford, adopted daughter of the late actress Joan Crawford, turned her lifetime of abuse at the hands of her famous mother into a creative outlet by writing the controversial book *Mommie Dearest* (1978, 1997). She was the first to go public with the tragedies of her life surrounding her adoption, but not the last. Her courage to expose her mother's violence and the system that allowed terrible things to happen has opened the door for many other adoptees to follow. Often, through creative expression, we are able to finally face the pain in our life and perhaps find the closure we need to move on.

Reunion, like all relationships, takes at least two consenting participants in order to make it work. If either one of the two is unwilling or unable to contribute their fair share to the relationship, then it won't be sustainable. A house divided will fall. If you find the walls of your reunion are tumbling down, what mortar can you use to reglue its foundation?

Start with apologies and ask for forgiveness if you need it. Move forward with the promise of open communication, inclusion on decision making, and empathy for the other person. Consult with a professional therapist either alone or together, in an effort to rebuild what was damaged. Take baby steps in the relationship. Don't take anything for granted. Realize that although you are dealing with a blood relative, this person is actually a stranger to you. Show them the same, if not more, respect than you would show a new friend.

Likewise, if you are the person who has become disenchanted with the reunion relationship, be honest with the other person. Your choices will be to either work toward repairing whatever caused you to become disillusioned, or respectfully disclosing to them your need for distance.

All of the information in these pages has been written to provide you the insight you will need to steer the course of your own reunion. Try not to mimic the reunions of other people whom you read about here, but rather draw from their experiences to help you forge your own unique reunion and avoid some of the universal pitfalls that can lead to a failed relationship.

Above all else, remember your reunion aerobics. Exercise caution, compassion, responsibility, and patience throughout your reunion workout. It will make you mentally fit and better prepared for anything that reunion might require of you.

Resources

National Organizations for Adoption Support and Reform

Contact the organizations listed below for complete information on membership, conferences, workshops, and available printed materials. Organizations with an asterisk (*) also maintain reunion registries. We recommend that you contact these groups independently for specific or detailed information.

*Adoptees Liberty Movement Association (ALMA)
P.O. Box 154—Washington Bridge Station
New York, NY 10033
(212) 581-1568

Adoptive Families of America (AFA)
3333 Highway 100 North
Minneapolis, MN 55422
(612) 535-4829

American Adoption Congress (AAC)
1000 Connecticut Avenue NW, #9
Washington, DC 20002
(202) 483-3399

*BigHugs
2503 Del Prado Blvd., #435
Cape Coral, FL 33904
1-800-BIG-HUGS

*Concerned United Birthparents, Inc. (CUB)
P.O. Box 230457
Encinitas, CA 92023

(800) 822-2777
email: info@cubirthparents.org

Council for Equal Rights in Adoption (CERA)
401 East 74th Street, Suite 17-D
New York, NY 10021-2919
(212) 988-0110

*International Soundex Reunion Registry (ISRR)
P. O. Box 2312
Carson City, NV 89702
(702) 882-7755

National Adoption Information Clearinghouse (NAIC)
330 C Street SW
Washington, DC 20002
888-251-0075

National Organization for Birthfathers and Adoption Reform
(NOBAR)
P.O. Box 50
Punta Gorda, FL 33951

North American Council on Adoptable Children (NACAC)
1821 University Avenue, Suite N-498
St. Paul, MN 55104
(612) 644-3036

North Carolina Center for Adoption Education (CAE)
P.O. Box 4153
Chapel Hill, NC 27515
(919) 967-5010

Resources for Adoptive Parents
4049 Brookside Avenue S.
Minneapolis, MN 55416
(612) 926-6959

Internet Support, Advocacy, and Reunion Registry Web Sites

The following organizations are a few who offer support, reform advocacy, or reunion registries via the Internet. There are over a thousand adoption-related Web sites on the Internet, making it impossible to list them all. Because Web site addresses change frequently, we apologize in advance if you attempt to contact one of these groups via the Internet and fail. If for some reason you are unable to connect online with one of the organizations represented below, try a search using the keyword "adoption," which may lead you to the Web addresses you need.

Adoptees and Birthparents for Open Records Nationally (ABORN)
www.aborn.org

Adoption by Choice
www.adoptionbychoice.com

The Adoption Connections Project: Women's Journeys
www.sover.net/~adopt/

Adoption Crossroads/Council for Equal Rights in Adoption (CERA)
www.adoptioncrossroads.org

Adoptive Parent Registry
www.adoptionregistry.com.

Adoption Search Center
http://www.adopteesearchcenter.org.

Adoption-Speak
www.netaxs.com/~sparky/adoption

American Adoption Congress
www.american-adoption-cong.org

Bastard Nation
www.bastardnation.org

BigHugs
www.reunionregistry.com

Birthfathers Support
www.parentsplace.com
e-mail: stafford@winternet.com

Birth Dad's Mailing List
e-mail: bfsupport-request@majordomo.net

Birthmom's Support List
http://bmom.net

Birthmother Heartstrings
www.geocities.com/Heartland/Trail/2074

Birthmother Search Resources
www.personal.riverusers.com/~oburt/birthmothers.html

Birthmother Support
http://members.tripod.com/~Heather256

Birth Parents—Adoption Net Links
www.adoptiontriad.org

Birthparents Searching
www.adopting.org/supporta.html

International Soundex Reunion Registry (ISRR)
www.regday.org

NAIC (National Adoption Information Clearinghouse)
www.adopting.org/impact.html

North Carolina Center for Adoption Education
www.adoptioneducationcenter.homestead.com/indexA.html

Sunflower Birthmother Support Group
www.bmom.net
e-mail: alanamil@aol.com

Foreign Search/Registry Services

Adoptees' Foreign Searches
P.O. Box 360074
Strongsville, OH 44136
(216) 238-1004

International Social Services
American Branch
390 Park Avenue South
New York, NY 10016
(212) 232-6350

Periodicals

Adopted Child
P.O. Box 9362
Moscow, ID 83843

Adoptive Families Magazine
333 Highway 100 North
Minneapolis, MN 55422

AdoptNet Magazine
P.O. Box 50514
Palo Alto, CA 94303-0514

CUB Communicator
P.O. Box 230457
Encinitas, CA 92023

The Decree
American Adoption Congress (AAC)
1000 Connecticut Avenue NW, #9
Washington, DC 20036

People Searching News
P.O. Box 100444
Palm Bay, FL 32910-0444

Roots and Wings
P.O. Box 638
Chester, NJ 07930

Suggested Reading

Aigner, Hal. 1992. *Adoption in America: Coming of Age.* Larkspur, Calif.: Paradigm Press.

Baran, Annette and Reuben Pannor. 1993. *Lethal Secrets: The Psychology of Donor Insemination.* New York: Amisted Press.

Benit, M.K. 1976. *The Politics of Adoption.* New York: Free Press.

Bradshaw, John. 1995. *Family Secrets: What You Don't Know Can Hurt You.* New York: Bantam Books.

Brodzinsky, David, Marshall Schechter, and Robin Henig. 1992. *Being Adopted: The Lifelong Search for Self.* New York: Doubleday.

Chamberlain, David. 1988. *Babies Remember Birth.* New York: Ballantine Books.

Chesler, P. 1988. *Sacred Bond: The Legacy of Baby M.* New York: Times Books.

Duprau, Jeanne. 1990. *Adoption: The Facts, Feelings and Issues of a Double Heritage.* New York: Julian Messner.

Gediman, Judith S., and Linda P. Brown. 1989. *Birthbond: Reunion Between Birthparents and Adoptees.* Far Hills, N.J.: New Horizon Press.

Gritter, James L., ed. 1989. *Adoption Without Fear.* San Antonio, Tex.: Corona Publishing CompaNew York.

Holt, Marilyn Irvin. 1992. *The Orphan Trains: Placing Out in America.* Lincoln, Neb.: University of Nebraska Press.

Kirk, H. David. 1981. *Adoptive Kinship.* Toronto, Canada: Butterworth Publishers.

Krementz, Jill. 1988. *How It Feels to Be Adopted.* New York: Alfred A. Knopf.

Lifton, Betty Jean. 1977. *Twice Born: Memoirs of an Adopted Daughter.* New York: Penguin Books.

———. 1979. *Lost and Found: The Adoption Experience.* New York: Dial Press.

McKay, Linda Back. 1998. *Shadow Mothers.* St. Cloud, Minn.: North Star Press of St. Cloud, Inc.

Musser, Sandra K. 1977. *I Would Have Searched Forever.* Coral Gables, Fla.: Adoption Awareness Press.

———. 1984. *What Kind of Love Is This?* Coral Gables, Fla.: Adoption Awareness Press.

———. 1996. *To Prison with Love.* Coral Gables, Fla.: Adoption Awareness Press.

Pavao, Joyce. 1998. *The Family of Adoption.* Boston, Mass.: Beacon Press.

Portnoy, Francie., MA. 1997. *One Wonderful You.* Greensboro, N.C.: Children's Home Society Publication.

Silber, K. and P. Speedlin. 1983. *Dear Birthmother.* San Antonio, Tex.: Corona Publishing CompaNew York.

Silber, K. and P. Dorner. 1990. *Children of Open Adoption.* San Antonio, Tex.: Corona Publishing CompaNew York.

Silverman, P. 1981. *Helping Women Cope with Grief.* New York: Saga Publications, Inc.

Solinger, Rickie. 1992. *Wake Up Little Susie: Single Pregnancy and Race Before Roe v. Wade.* New York: Routledge.

Soll, Joe. 2000. *Adoption Healing: A Path to Recovery.* Baltimore, Md.: Gateway Press, Inc.

Strauss, Jean. 1994. *Birthright: A Guide to Search and Reunion for Adoptees, Birthparents and Adoptive Parents.* New York: Penguin USA.

Taylor, Patricia E. 1995. *Shadow Train.* Baltimore, Md.: Gateway Press, Inc.

References

ABC Television Network. May 1999. *20/20:* "Mothers in the Shadows." New York.

Andersen, Robert. 1993. *Second Choice: Growing Up Adopted.* St. Louis, Mo.: Badgerhill Press.

Bailey, Julie Jarrell. 1995. *Didn't Know.* Workshop: The Birth Mother's Tribute. Southeastern Regional Conference on Adoption, Atlantic Beach, N.C.

———. 1998. *When Life Separates.* Chapel Hill, N.C.: MOTH Publishing

Chamberlain, David. 1988. *Babies Remember Birth.* New York: Ballantine Books.

Child Welfare League. 1965. *Perspectives on Adoption Research.* Washington, D.C.

Council for Equal Rights in Adoption. 1997. Position Paper. Ckongers, N.Y.: CERA.

Crawford, Christina. 1978, 1997. *Mommie Dearest.* Moscow, Idaho: Seven Springs Press.

Garland, K. 1986. *Grief: The Transitional Process.* The Journal of Neonatal Nursing 5:3. December. Published by the National Association of Neonatal Nurses.

Giddens, N. Lynn. 1983. *Faces of Adoption.* Chapel Hill, N.C.: Amberly Publications.

———. 1998. *Post-Traumatic Stress Disorder Symptoms in Birthmothers.* Master's Thesis. Montpelier, Vt.: Norwich University.

Kubler-Ross, Elisabeth. 1968. *On Death and Dying.* New York: Macmillan Company.

Lifton, Betty Jean. 1994. *Journey of the Adopted Self: A Quest for Wholeness*. New York: Basic Books.

Matsakis, Aphrodite. 1996. *I Can't Get Over It: A Handbook for Trauma Survivors*. Oakland, Calif.: New Harbinger Publications.

Portnoy, Francie. 1998. Two Family Legacies. *Adoptive Families of America Magazine*. January/February Edition.

————. 1997. *One Wonderful You*. Greensboro, N.C.: Children's Home Society of North Carolina.

Schaefer, Carol. 1991. *The Other Mother*. New York: Soho Press.

Sorosky, Arthur D., Annette Baran, and Reuben Pannor. 1978. *The Adoption Triangle*. New York: Anchor Press/Doubleday.

Stiffler, LaVonne Harper. 1992. *Synchronicity and Reunion: The Genetic Connection of Adoptees and Birthparents*. Hobe Sound, Fla.: FEA Publishing.

University of Minnesota Psychology Department Web Page. 1999.

Verrier, Nancy Newton. 1993. *The Primal Wound*. Baltimore, Md.: Gateway Press.

Westberg, G. E. 1997. *Good Grief*. Thirty-fifth Anniversary Edition. Minneapolis, Minn.: Fortress Press.

Julie Jarrell Bailey is Cofounder of the North Carolina Center for Adoption Education and serves on the Board of Directors for the Mandala Adoption Agency in Chapel Hill. She is also a parent-to-parent volunteer with the North Carolina Family Support Network, a trained Hospice volunteer, an adoption peer counselor and substitute teacher in the public school system. Julie has served as an advocate lobbyist in adoption reform for the State of North Carolina and has been a workshop leader and facilitator for adoption conferences at the national, state, and regional levels since 1994. She has worked as a professional writer since 1970 and in recent years focused her talents on adoption-related topics. Julie has been a reunited birth mother since 1996, and she holds the unique status of having adopted her birth daughter two years post-reunion. She is also the adoptive mother of three special needs brothers who joined the Bailey family ranks in 1996. She has been married to her husband, Steve, since 1976. After living most of her life in Central Florida, Julie relocated with Steve to the serenity of North Carolina to become adoptive parents and involve themselves in adoption reform issues.

Lynn N. Giddens, M.A., and Ph.D. candidate, is the Founder of the North Carolina Adoption Connections Reunion Registry and Cofounder of the North Carolina Center for Adoption Education in Chapel Hill. She currently serves as the North Carolina Representative to the American Adoption Congress in Washington, D.C., and she has been a workshop presenter at adoption conferences across the country, as well as a conference coordinator. In addition to being an adult adoptee who was reunited with her birth family over 20 years ago, Lynn has been the driving force behind legislative reform in North Carolina adoption laws since 1980. She also works as a teacher of special needs students in the public school system.

Annette Baran, M.S.W., is one of the pioneers in the field of modern adoption. As coauthor of *Adoption Triangle*, the first book to advocate opening sealed records, she helped to bring about significant changes in the institution of adoption and influenced the practice of agencies throughout the world. Her career has included clinical and administrative work in adoption agencies, teaching and training, research and writing, expert witnessing, consultation, and the private practice of psychotherapy. She is also coauthor of *Lethal Secrets*, the first book to examine the emotional aspects of donor insemination and other alternative methods of reproduction. Other writings include chapters in the *Encyclopedia of Bioethics, The Psychology of Adoption, Adolescent Psychiatry*, and many magazine and journal articles. As a recognized expert, she has appeared on many television shows and documentaries, acted as keynote speaker at conferences, and lectured in foreign universities.

Some Other New Harbinger Self-Help Titles

Family Guide to Emotional Wellness, $24.95
Undefended Love, $13.95
The Great Big Book of Hope, $15.95
Don't Leave it to Chance, $13.95
Emotional Claustrophobia, $12.95
The Relaxation & Stress Reduction Workbook, Fifth Edition, $19.95
The Loneliness Workbook, $14.95
Thriving with Your Autoimmune Disorder, $16.95
Illness and the Art of Creative Self-Expression, $13.95
The Interstitial Cystitis Survival Guide, $14.95
Outbreak Alert, $15.95
Don't Let Your Mind Stunt Your Growth, $10.95
Energy Tapping, $14.95
Under Her Wing, $13.95
Self-Esteem, Third Edition, $15.95
Women's Sexualitites, $15.95
Knee Pain, $14.95
Helping Your Anxious Child, $12.95
Breaking the Bonds of Irritable Bowel Syndrome, $14.95
Multiple Chemical Sensitivity: A Survival Guide, $16.95
Dancing Naked, $14.95
Why Are We Still Fighting, $15.95
From Sabotage to Success, $14.95
Parkinson's Disease and the Art of Moving, $15.95
A Survivor's Guide to Breast Cancer, $13.95
Men, Women, and Prostate Cancer, $15.95
Make Every Session Count: Getting the Most Out of Your Brief Therapy, $10.95
Virtual Addiction, $12.95
After the Breakup, $13.95
Why Can't I Be the Parent I Want to Be?, $12.95
The Secret Message of Shame, $13.95
The OCD Workbook, $18.95
Tapping Your Inner Strength, $13.95
Binge No More, $14.95
When to Forgive, $12.95
Practical Dreaming, $12.95
Healthy Baby, Toxic World, $15.95
Making Hope Happen, $14.95
I'll Take Care of You, $12.95
Survivor Guilt, $14.95
Children Changed by Trauma, $13.95
Understanding Your Child's Sexual Behavior, $12.95
The Self-Esteem Companion, $10.95
The Gay and Lesbian Self-Esteem Book, $13.95
Making the Big Move, $13.95
How to Survive and Thrive in an Empty Nest, $13.95
Living Well with a Hidden Disability, $15.95
Overcoming Repetitive Motion Injuries the Rossiter Way, $15.95
What to Tell the Kids About Your Divorce, $13.95
The Divorce Book, Second Edition, $15.95
Claiming Your Creative Self: True Stories from the Everyday Lives of Women, $15.95
Taking Control of TMJ, $13.95
Winning Against Relapse: A Workbook of Action Plans for Recurring Health and Emotional Problems, $14.95
Facing 30: Women Talk About Constructing a Real Life and Other Scary Rites of Passage, $12.95
The Worry Control Workbook, $15.95
Wanting What You Have: A Self-Discovery Workbook, $18.95
When Perfect Isn't Good Enough: Strategies for Coping with Perfectionism, $13.95
Earning Your Own Respect: A Handbook of Personal Responsibility, $12.95
High on Stress: A Woman's Guide to Optimizing the Stress in Her Life, $13.95
Infidelity: A Survival Guide, $13.95
Stop Walking on Eggshells, $14.95
Consumer's Guide to Psychiatric Drugs, $16.95
The Fibromyalgia Advocate: Getting the Support You Need to Cope with Fibromyalgia and Myofascial Pain, $18.95
Working Anger: Preventing and Resolving Conflict on the Job, $12.95
Healthy Living with Diabetes, $13.95
Better Boundries: Owning and Treasuring Your Life, $13.95
Goodbye Good Girl, $12.95
Fibromyalgia & Chronic Myofascial Pain Syndrome, $19.95
The Depression Workbook: Living With Depression and Manic Depression, $17.95

Call **toll free, 1-800-748-6273,** or log on to our online bookstore at **www.newharbinger.com** to order. Have your Visa or Mastercard number ready. Or send a check for the titles you want to New Harbinger Publications, Inc., 5674 Shattuck Ave., Oakland, CA 94609. Include $3.80 for the first book and 75¢ for each additional book, to cover shipping and handling. (California residents please include appropriate sales tax.) Allow two to five weeks for delivery.

Prices subject to change without notice.